National Textbook Company

ECONOMICS

Content Review Workbook

J. Holton Wilson
Professor
Central Michigan University

&

J.R. Clark
Probasco Chair
University of
Tennessee/Chattanooga

National Textbook Company
a division of NTC/CONTEMPORARY PUBLISHING GROUP
Lincolnwood, Illinois USA

ISBN: 0-538-65596-8
ISBN: 0-538-92855-7

Published by National Textbook Company,
a division of NTC/Contemporary Publishing Group, Inc.
4255 West Touhy Avenue,
Lincolnwood, (Chicago) Illinois 60712-1975 U.S.A.
© 1997 NTC/Contemporary Publishing Group, Inc.

6 7 8 9 10   MZ   09 08 07 06

CONTENTS

The Economic Way of Thinking

Part 1 — Building Your Economic Vocabulary

Directions: Complete each of the following sentences with chapter vocabulary from the list below.

allocation
budget constraint
economics
economic system
limited resources
macroeconomics

microeconomics
opportunity benefit
opportunity cost
scarcity
theory
unlimited wants and needs

1. Limited resources available to satisfy unlimited wants and needs create _____.

2. Because we never feel that all our wants and needs are satisfied, economists say that we have _____.

3. We say that we have _____ because there is only so much wood, glass, concrete, and steel available to produce goods.

4. _____ is the process of choosing which needs will be satisfied and how much of our resources we will use to satisfy them.

5. _____ is the social science concerned with how society allocates its scarce resources among its unlimited wants and needs.

6. The cost of giving up one alternative to acquire another is the _____.

7. _____ is the gain received by making a particular choice.

8. The study of the choices of individuals concerning one firm, one product, or one industry in the economy is referred to as _____.

9. _____ is the branch of economics that examines the behavior of the whole economy at once.

10. An _____ is the combination of social and individual decision making a society uses to answer the three economic questions.

11. A _____ is a way of describing reality in a simplified way.

12. Trying to decide how many $5 books and $1 magazines can be purchased with an income of $20 is an example of a _____.

Part 2 — Checking Your Economic Knowledge

Directions: Carefully read the following statements. Decide whether the statement is *True* or *False*. Fill in the answer bubble for **T** for *True* or **F** for *False*. If any part of the statement is *False,* then the statement is *False.*

1. Scarcity comes about because, although resources are unlimited in this world, the wants and needs of individuals are highly limited. . . . .   ( )T   ( )F

2. Human wants and needs are unlimited because, as soon as we satisfy one type of need such as food or shelter, we have the ability to realize or even invent some new ones such as safety or personal satisfaction. . . . .   ( )T   ( )F

3. Scarcity is the major reason it is necessary to allocate our resources among our wants and needs. . . . .   ( )T   ( )F

4. Every choice has both an opportunity cost and an opportunity benefit. . . . .   ( )T   ( )F

5. It is rational for decision makers to choose an alternative for which the opportunity benefit is greater than the opportunity cost. . . . .   ( )T   ( )F

6. Microeconomics is the branch of economics that examines individuals' choices concerning one product, one firm, or one industry. It deals mostly with individual decision making. . . . .   ( )T   ( )F

7. Macroeconomics is the branch of economics that examines the behavior of the entire economy at once. . . . .   ( )T   ( )F

8. Regardless of their type of decision-making process, all economies must answer the basic economic questions of what to produce, how to produce, and when to produce goods and services. . . . .   ( )T   ( )F

9. The major reason economic theory is important is that it presents a picture of reality with every detail for us to see. . . . .   ( )T   ( )F

10. Economic theory is much like a road map and is precise in almost all situations. .   ( )T   ( )F

Part 3 — Mastering Economic Concepts

Directions: Carefully read the following items. Fill in the answer bubble next to the letter of the *best* answer.

1. A knowledge of economics is vital to students because **(a)** it directly affects the course of their everyday lives **(b)** it helps them make informed decisions in both the marketplace and the voting booth **(c)** it makes them more effective citizens **(d)** all of these . . .   ( )a   ( )b   ( )c   ( )d

2. Economics is a science that analyzes **(a)** how people get rich **(b)** how to hit it big in the stock market **(c)** how the government spends our tax dollars **(d)** how individuals and societies make choices . . . .   ( )a   ( )b   ( )c   ( )d

3. Scarcity is the basic economic problem. Scarcity comes about because **(a)** people's wants and needs are limited while the resources to fulfill those needs are unlimited **(b)** human beings always want more money **(c)** people's wants and needs are unlimited while the resources to fulfill those needs are limited **(d)** sometimes there is not enough of everything to go around . . .   ( )a   ( )b   ( )c   ( )d

4. Economists and other social scientists contend that human wants and needs are unlimited. By this they mean **(a)** humans are selfish and unreasonable **(b)** as soon as one need is satisfied we invent another **(c)** there is just not enough of everything to go around **(d)** none of these . . . .   ( )a ( )b ( )c ( )d

5. Resources in the economic sense of the word are **(a)** money and checks **(b)** land, timber, and iron ore **(c)** anything used to satisfy wants and needs **(d)** things we use to build or make something . .   ( )a ( )b ( )c ( )d

6. If your income were unlimited, you would **(a)** not be affected by scarcity **(b)** be affected very little by scarcity **(c)** still be affected by scarcity since some resources such as your time would still be limited **(d)** none of these . . . .   ( )a ( )b ( )c ( )d

7. Economics is one of the **(a)** physical sciences **(b)** social sciences **(c)** mathematical sciences **(d)** theological sciences . . . .   ( )a ( )b ( )c ( )d

8. Imagine that you are about to choose how you will spend Saturday evening this week. Your opportunities are spending $25 to go out on a date or studying for your economics exam. If you choose to study, your opportunity cost is **(a)** $25 **(b)** insufficient information given **(c)** a date **(d)** there is no opportunity cost in this case . . . .   ( )a ( )b ( )c ( )d

9. If you choose to mow your neighbor's lawn next Saturday for the $10 fee that is promised to you, you will not be able to spend that same day at the lake. The opportunity benefit of this choice is **(a)** the $10 fee **(b)** a day at the lake **(c)** there is no opportunity benefit in this case **(d)** a day at the lake and the $10 fee . . . .   ( )a ( )b ( )c ( )d

10. The existence of scarcity means that we must make choices in allocating our resources. In every choice there is **(a)** an opportunity cost **(b)** the cost of giving up an alternative **(c)** some opportunity that we cannot enjoy at the same time **(d)** all of these . . . .   ( )a ( )b ( )c ( )d

11. All societies must make choices. These choices are made by **(a)** individuals in the marketplace **(b)** whole societies through the voting process **(c)** both individuals and whole societies **(d)** kings and dictators only. . . . .   ( )a ( )b ( )c ( )d

12. Microeconomics is that branch of economics concerned primarily with **(a)** social choice by the whole society **(b)** individual choice by members of the society **(c)** both social and individual choices **(d)** all of these . . . .   ( )a ( )b ( )c ( )d

13. Macroeconomics is that branch of economics concerned primarily with **(a)** social choices by the whole society **(b)** individual choices by members of the whole society **(c)** both individual and social choices **(d)** scarcity of resources . . . .   ( )a ( )b ( )c ( )d

14. The three basic questions that all economies must decide upon are **(a)** where, how, and when to produce **(b)** what, how, and when to produce **(c)** what, how, and for whom to produce **(d)** what, why, and how to produce. . . . .   ( )a ( )b ( )c ( )d

15. In the U.S. economy, the decision of what to produce is made **(a)** by individual consumers and sellers **(b)** by government employees only **(c)** by individuals acting as consumers **(d)** by individuals acting as suppliers . . . .   ( )a ( )b ( )c ( )d

16. In the U.S. economy, the question for whom to produce is made primarily by **(a)** government **(b)** individuals acting as consumers, producers, and voters **(c)** workers **(d)** the entire society through voting . . . .   ( )a ( )b ( )c ( )d

17. In a market economy, the three basic economic questions are answered primarily **(a)** in the marketplace **(b)** by the government **(c)** in the voting booth **(d)** in both the marketplace and the voting booth. . . . .   ( )a ( )b ( )c ( )d

18. In a command economy, the three basic economic questions are answered primarily **(a)** by the government **(b)** in the marketplace **(c)** in the voting booth **(d)** in both the marketplace and the voting booth. . . . .   ( )a ( )b ( )c ( )d

19. Economic theory is important to study because **(a)** it simplifies reality **(b)** it helps us to make informed decisions **(c)** it is relevant to our everyday choices **(d)** all of these . . . .   ( )a ( )b ( )c ( )d

Making Individual Decisions

Part 1 — Building Your Economic Vocabulary

Directions: Complete the following word puzzle by using the definitions to identify the key terms from this chapter. Circle each word as you find it. Words may read in any direction: forward, backward, vertically, horizontally, or on the diagonal. Item 0 has been completed for you.

```
W  A  P  U  A  D  O  F  L  F  O  F  O  T  T (I
S  U  S  T  P  E  F  E  C  X  A  I  L  F  Q  N
T  O  Y  T  I  L  I  T  U  J  L  T  B  A  U  D
D  E  C  I  S  I  O  N  M  A  T  R  I  X  A  I
I  V  H  T  M  N  C  U  E  R  E  Q  U  E  Z  V
Y  I  I  I  A  M  O  D  E  L  R  K  A  P  L  I
T  T  C  F  R  L  A  X  N  B  N  M  C  B  H  D
I  N  I  O  K  A  P  L  D  U  A  A  Y  E  D  U
V  E  N  R  E  U  Q  S  M  Z  T  T  R  N  I  A
I  C  C  P  T  D  X  I  C  O  I  I  A  E  X  L
T  N  O  C  E  O  N  I  V  C  V  H  L  N  Y  C
C  I  M  I  C  I  L  G  R  E  E  L  G  I  L  H
E  C  E  M  O  Y  J  A  S  L  D  C  O  C  N  O
J  I  T  O  N  T  C  O  B  J  E  T  I  O  F  I
B  M  H  N  O  S  M  I  L  O  E  V  K  T  E  C
O  O  O  O  M  L  S  K  E  R  F  R  B  O  Y  E)
M  N  R  C  Y  I  E  C  O  N  O  M  Y  T  R  E
E  O  D  E  V  T  A  A  J  W  E  M  O  P  I  N
I  C  O  N  E  U  S  T  A  I  R  E  T  I  R  C
E  E  I  P  R  E  F  W  N  A  Y  L  I  T  U  E
```

0. the decisions made by people acting separately

1. an economy in which the economic questions are decided mostly by individuals in the marketplace

2. the increase in our personal satisfaction that may result from some economic activity

3. the nonmonetary reward we receive from taking some action

4. the difference between the money you obtain from selling a product and the cost of producing the product

5. the incentive for individuals to choose in the best interest of society by pursuing their own self-interest

6. a simplified form of reality that shows the relationship between different factors

7. ruling out those aspects of a problem that seem important only because of strong emotions or feelings about them

8. a possible course of action

9. the characteristics of a group of alternatives that will be judged to make a choice

10. a table comparing possible decisions

11. the satisfaction one receives from the consumption, use, or ownership of a good or service

12. the unit of measurement for utility

Part 2 — Checking Your Economic Knowledge

Directions: Carefully read the following statements. Decide whether the statement is *True* or *False*. Fill in the answer bubble for **T** for *True* or **F** for *False*. If any part of the statement is *False*, then the statement is *False*.

1. In market economies, the economic question of what to produce is decided primarily by consumers voting with their dollars in the marketplace. . . . . ( )T ( )F

2. Psychic income is the difference between the money you obtain from selling a product and the cost of producing the product. . . . . ( )T ( )F

3. Individual choice and self-interest are the two major forces behind a market economy. They create the drive for individuals to work hard, which benefits the whole society. . . . . ( )T ( )F

4. When producers and consumers trade in the marketplace, it is reasonably clear that the producer (seller) must gain and the consumer (buyer) must lose. . . . . . . ( )T ( )F

5. Adam Smith was the originator of the concept of the invisible hand which stated that, unless government regulates them, markets will not function efficiently. . . . . ( )T ( )F

6. Social choices can sometimes overpower individual choices and can reduce the incentive for self-interest and discourage individual productive efforts. . . . . ( )T ( )F

7. In order to make an effective personal decision, you should first define the problem. . . . . ( )T ( )F

8. When defining a problem, thinking objectively is important. . . . . ( )T ( )F

9. Having defined the problem in a personal decision, you should next list the alternatives available and the criteria on which you will evaluate each alternative. . . . . ( )T ( )F

10. The last two steps in effective personal decision making are to evaluate the alternatives in regard to your criteria and then to discuss the matter with your parents and friends. . . . . ( )T ( )F

11. Intelligent decisions are those that minimize the utility of the choice. . . . . ( )T ( )F

Part 3 — Mastering Economic Concepts

Directions: Carefully read the following items. Fill in the answer bubble next to the letter of the *best* answer.

1. Adam Smith was a Scottish economist who felt that
   (a) government should control business activity **(b)** the interests of the whole society were best served by each individual pursuing his or her own self-interest **(c)** trade guilds were in the best interest of individuals **(d)** government should support trade guilds and unions . . . .   ( )a ( )b ( )c ( )d

2. An individual choice is generally the preferred choice of **(a)** a group of individuals **(b)** people acting separately from one another **(c)** a society choosing as a whole **(d)** none of these . . . . . .   ( )a ( )b ( )c ( )d

3. Economic incentive is the **(a)** decrease in personal satisfaction that may result from some economic activity **(b)** increase in personal satisfaction that may result from some economic activity **(c)** economic question decided by individuals in a marketplace **(d)** force that guides individuals to choose in the best interest of society by pursuing their own self-interests. . . . .   ( )a ( )b ( )c ( )d

4. In a market economy, the question of what to produce is decided mostly by **(a)** consumers voting in the marketplace with their dollars **(b)** central planning by government **(c)** the cost of resources **(d)** all of these . . . .   ( )a ( )b ( )c ( )d

5. Farmers decide what process to use to grow wheat based upon **(a)** the cost of the different possible processes **(b)** the process that gives them the greatest profits **(c)** the process that benefits them the most **(d)** all of these. . . . .   ( )a ( )b ( )c ( )d

6. In the U.S. economy, the decision of who shall get the goods and services that are produced is made primarily by **(a)** individual consumers based upon what they can afford **(b)** the government based upon what it thinks we need **(c)** producers based upon what they want us to have **(d)** the directors of the Social Security system . . . .   ( )a ( )b ( )c ( )d

7. If the basic economic choices of what, how, and for whom to produce were made in the U.S. economy by individuals, the guiding force behind those choices would be **(a)** profit minimization **(b)** self-interest **(c)** tax laws **(d)** none of these . . . . . .   ( )a ( )b ( )c ( )d

8. In economics, the concept of self-interest means that people **(a)** are only interested in themselves **(b)** devote more effort and interest to those things that benefit them directly **(c)** are primarily interested in helping others **(d)** help others because it is to their own benefit . . . .   ( )a ( )b ( )c ( )d

9. Individual choice and self-interest create strong incentives for individuals to **(a)** work hard and benefit from their own decisions **(b)** steal from one another **(c)** work less than their coworkers **(d)** find the easiest way to do something . . . .   ( )a ( )b ( )c ( )d

10. Adam Smith's concept of the invisible hand means that people will do the greatest good for the whole society by **(a)** pursuing their own self-interest **(b)** always trying to do what is best for others **(c)** always doing what the government says is right **(d)** trying to look out for themselves and others. . . . .   ( )a ( )b ( )c ( )d

11. In Adam Smith's way of thinking, social choice reduced the incentives for **(a)** people to steal **(b)** people to think **(c)** people to work in their own self-interest **(d)** government to tax . . . .   ( )a ( )b ( )c ( )d

12. One way to make better individual decisions is to **(a)** consult with your friends and follow their advice **(b)** apply the five-step decision-making model **(c)** choose the alternative with the least points on a decision matrix **(d)** none of these . . . .   ( )a ( )b ( )c ( )d

13. One of the first steps to making a reasoned and well-thought-out choice is to **(a)** consider the other problems you may have **(b)** make a list of things you need to do **(c)** define the problem **(d)** none of these . . . .   ( )a ( )b ( )c ( )d

14. The second step to making a reasoned and well-thought-out choice is to **(a)** make a list of alternatives from which to choose **(b)** make a list of definitions for your problem **(c)** evaluate your criteria **(d)** assign points to the alternatives. . . . .   ( )a ( )b ( )c ( )d

15. When you have completed steps one and two of the decision process, you should next **(a)** list your alternatives **(b)** list your objectives **(c)** assign points to the alternatives **(d)** list the criteria by which you should evaluate your alternatives . . . .   ( )a ( )b ( )c ( )d

16. When you begin to evaluate your alternatives, you should **(a)** consider each alternative in regard to your criteria **(b)** consider each criteria in regard to each alternative **(c)** evaluate each consideration in regard to the objectives, criteria, alternatives, and goals **(d)** none of these . . . .   ( )a ( )b ( )c ( )d

17. The final step in making a well-reasoned and informed choice is to **(a)** choose the best criteria **(b)** choose the best objective **(c)** choose the best alternative **(d)** none of these. . . . .   ( )a ( )b ( )c ( )d

18. The organized and reasoned approach to decision making that you have studied helps you make better choices because it helps you clearly understand **(a)** the opportunity costs and benefits of each alternative you have to choose from **(b)** the good and bad things about some choices **(c)** the benefits of each choice you make **(d)** the opportunity costs of a choice . . . .   ( )a ( )b ( )c ( )d

19. In economics, psychic income means **(a)** utility or satisfaction aside from receiving money that a person gets from some activity **(b)** dollars paid to people for their mental abilities or intelligence **(c)** pride, personality, and perseverance **(d)** none of these . . . .   ( )a ( )b ( )c ( )d

Making Social Decisions

Part 1 — Building Your Economic Vocabulary

Directions: Match the following terms with the definitions below.

A. distribution effect
B. economies of scale
C. equity
D. freedom of choice
E. free rider
F. public goods

G. public goods rationale
H. social benefits
I. social choice
J. social costs
K. social economy
L. social goals

_____ 1. an economy in which the major economic questions are determined by the government representing the interests of the entire society

_____ 2. decision making by government in the interest of society

_____ 3. equality of opportunity

_____ 4. goods and services available to the whole society

_____ 5. the concept that some economic activities become more efficient when done on a large scale

_____ 6. the argument that some public goods can be produced more efficiently by social choice

_____ 7. a person who benefits from a public good without sharing its cost

_____ 8. the way the inconvenience of a social issue is spread among the members of the society

_____ 9. the goals of an entire society

_____ 10. the costs to a society of a social choice

_____ 11. the individual power to choose and receive both the costs and the benefits of a choice

_____ 12. the benefits received by a society from a social choice

Part 2 — Checking Your Economic Knowledge

Directions: Carefully read the following statements. Decide whether the statement is *True* or *False*. Fill in the answer bubble for **T** for *True* or **F** for *False*. If any part of the statement is *False*, then the statement is *False*.

1. In a social economy, the questions of what, how, and for whom to produce are decided primarily by social choice through a central planning committee. . . . .   ( )T ( )F

2. In a planned economy, producers often go out of business when they fail to produce what consumers want. . . . .   ( )T ( )F

3. In economies where social choice is the guiding factor, the incentives to work hard in your own self-interest are very strong. . . . .   ( )T ( )F

4. Planned or social economies attempt to distribute the goods and services produced in the economy in an equitable way. . . . .   ( )T ( )F

5. Karl Marx believed that capitalism would eventually evolve into communism, a classless society where everyone was equal. . . . .   ( )T ( )F

6. A major advantage of public goods provided through social choice is that they spread their very large costs over all members of the society. . . . .   ( )T ( )F

7. Public goods are of such a nature that it is difficult to exclude some members of the society from their use. This is known as the free rider problem. . . . .   ( )T ( )F

8. When persons are selected to make decisions for the entire society, it is important for them to clarify the social costs and social benefits of each choice to their constituents. . . . .   ( )T ( )F

9. In making an effective social choice, a society should define the problem, list the alternatives, list the criteria, and select the central planning agency that will make the decisions. . . . .   ( )T ( )F

10. Even the most carefully made social decisions frequently take away freedom of choice. . . . .   ( )T ( )F

Part 3 — Mastering Economic Concepts

Directions: Carefully read the following items. Fill in the answer bubble next to the letter of the *best* answer.

1. In a social economy such as China, the question of what goods and services will be produced is determined by **(a)** the central planning committee **(b)** the department of production **(c)** consumers and producers choosing together **(d)** voters designated to choose this year's output . . . .   ( )a ( )b ( )c ( )d

2. In a social economy, the question of what resources will be used in production is decided by **(a)** individual producers guided by the price of resources **(b)** all producers deciding together **(c)** the central planning committee **(d)** producers and the central planning committee together . . . .   ( )a ( )b ( )c ( )d

3. In a social economy, producers have strong incentives to produce those goods that **(a)** meet consumers' needs **(b)** the consumers will buy **(c)** government directs them to produce **(d)** consumers and government tell them they should produce . . . .   ( )a ( )b ( )c ( )d

4. Once goods are produced in a social economy, they are at least theoretically distributed in such a way as to provide **(a)** equity—an equal share for almost everyone **(b)** efficiency—distributed to those who will put the goods to their best use **(c)** a higher standard of living for everyone **(d)** a minimum standard of living for everyone . . . .   ( )a ( )b ( )c ( )d

5. Karl Marx was an early advocate of **(a)** socialist economics **(b)** market economies **(c)** capitalism **(d)** individual decision making . . . .   ( )a ( )b ( )c ( )d

6. Of the following goods and services, the ones that could best be provided as public goods are **(a)** steel, lumber, and food **(b)** buses, airline tickets, and automobiles **(c)** movies, vacations, and clothes **(d)** police protection, a court system, and fire protection . . . .   ( )a ( )b ( )c ( )d

7. In the United States, we make some of our economic choices as social choices. We sometimes decide to build roads, schools, and parks or provide national defense. We make these choices as social decisions because of **(a)** the public goods rationale **(b)** economies of scale **(c)** both (a) and (b) **(d)** none of these . . . . .   ( )a ( )b ( )c ( )d

8. The public goods rationale is based upon the concept that **(a)** the public should provide goods to the poor **(b)** all goods can be provided more cheaply as public goods **(c)** some goods can be provided more efficiently and cheaply as public goods **(d)** goods cannot be provided to the public unless everyone pays an equal share . . . .   ( )a ( )b ( )c ( )d

9. It is important to enforce social decisions with the power of law to **(a)** avoid the free rider problem **(b)** spread the costs of social decisions over the whole society **(c)** both (a) and (b) **(d)** none of these . . . .   ( )a ( )b ( )c ( )d

10. In the United States, we make our social decisions by **(a)** voting for candidates who know the most about economics and social decisions **(b)** how we spend our dollars in the marketplace **(c)** voting for honest politicians **(d)** voting for officials who most closely reflect our views on the issues . . . .   ( )a ( )b ( )c ( )d

11. We can improve the quality of the social decisions we make by **(a)** TV **(b)** applying the five-step decision-making process to our social decisions **(c)** using social decisions to modify the decision-making process **(d)** considering alternative candidates . . . .   ( )a ( )b ( )c ( )d

12. In the social decision-making process, social goals are very much like **(a)** both the criteria and alternatives of the individual decision-making process **(b)** the alternatives we use to evaluate the criteria in the individual decision-making process **(c)** the criteria we set up to evaluate alternatives in the individual decision-making process **(d)** none of these . . . .   ( )a ( )b ( )c ( )d

13. A social cost is the **(a)** cost to individuals affected by a social decision **(b)** cost to society for any given individual choice **(c)** physical cost of producing goods that benefit society **(d)** cost to society for any given social choice. . . . .   ( )a ( )b ( )c ( )d

14. Social benefits are **(a)** the total benefits received by individuals from a social choice **(b)** the total benefits received by the government from a social choice **(c)** the total benefits received by the entire society from a social choice **(d)** freedom to receive the costs and benefits of a choice . . . .   ( )a ( )b ( )c ( )d

15. Elected officials in the United States who make social choices have completed only part of their jobs when the choice is made. Their next most important task is to **(a)** see that the benefits are spread evenly throughout all of society **(b)** clearly communicate why and how they made their decision **(c)** make decisions based on their personal values alone **(d)** correct any mistakes that may have been made. . . . .   ( )a ( )b ( )c ( )d

Private Sector Decisions

Part 1 — Building Your Economic Vocabulary

Directions: Complete the following crossword puzzle with vocabulary terms from this chapter.

ACROSS

1. the part of an economy that is owned by individuals and is operated for their personal benefit
6. the giving of one thing in return for some other thing
7. the part of an economy that is owned by and operated for the benefit of the whole society
9. individuals who take the risk of producing a product for a profit

DOWN

1. a system in which individuals take the risk of producing goods or services to make a profit
2. costs or benefits passed on outside of the market system
3. the rivalry between two or more parties to gain benefits from a third party
4. achieving the maximum benefit from a given amount and combination of resources
5. goods that are privately owned and used to benefit only their owners
8. exchange activities between buyers and sellers of goods and services

 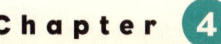

Part 2 — Checking Your Economic Knowledge

Directions: Carefully read the following statements. Decide whether the statement is *True* or *False*. Fill in the answer bubble for **T** for *True* or **F** for *False*. If any part of the statement is *False*, then the statement is *False*.

1. The private sector of the economy is that part of our economy that is owned by and operated for the benefit of all individuals. . . . . ( )T ( )F

2. Private ownership entitles the owners to receive the benefits of whatever they own and to exclude others from those benefits if they so desire. . . . . ( )T ( )F

3. In the private sector, it is expected that individuals will choose that alternative that produces the maximum private benefit or the minimum private cost to them. . . . . ( )T ( )F

4. Equity is the primary concern of the private sector. . . . . ( )T ( )F

5. One factor that forces the private sector to be more efficient in the production of private goods is the existence of competition. . . . . ( )T ( )F

6. Competition among producers in the marketplace works to the consumer's advantage. . . . . ( )T ( )F

7. One major contribution markets make to the economic process is the supplying of valuable price information. . . . . ( )T ( )F

8. One major drawback of markets is that they seldom provide many choices among which the consumer may choose. . . . . ( )T ( )F

9. Entrepreneurs are individuals who bring together the inputs of production to produce goods or services to satisfy consumers' wants and needs at a profit. . . . ( )T ( )F

10. A major problem entrepreneurs face in the marketplace is that they must take risks. . . . . ( )T ( )F

11. The existence of some public goods such as roads or national defense definitely helps markets function more efficiently. . . . . ( )T ( )F

12. The private sector sometimes passes costs on to the entire society in the form of externalities such as pollution. . . . . ( )T ( )F

Part 3 — Mastering Economic Concepts

Directions: Carefully read the following items. Fill in the answer bubble next to the letter of the *best* answer.

1. The private sector of our economy is defined as **(a)** government at all levels of our economy and the institutions it creates to help our economy function **(b)** all real estate that is privately owned **(c)** all personal property owned by individuals **(d)** that portion of our economy owned by and operated for the benefit of private individuals . . . . ( )a ( )b ( )c ( )d

2. If you own your own property, you have the right to **(a)** occupy that property and keep others out **(b)** enjoy all the benefits of that property yourself **(c)** sell that property to another for a profit or loss **(d)** all of these. . . . . ( )a ( )b ( )c ( )d

3. The major difference between the private and public sector is **(a)** individuals can be excluded from the benefits of the public sector but not the private sector **(b)** individuals cannot be excluded from the benefits of the public sector but can be excluded from the benefits of the private sector **(c)** the private sector is owned by all citizens while the public sector is privately owned **(d)** only the public sector pays taxes .... ( )a ( )b ( )c ( )d

4. The private sector is primarily controlled by **(a)** public decision makers **(b)** public and individual decision makers **(c)** individual choice **(d)** government .... ( )a ( )b ( )c ( )d

5. In the private sector, individuals try to **(a)** maximize public benefits **(b)** maximize tax revenues **(c)** maximize individual benefits **(d)** maximize the benefits of their neighbors .... ( )a ( )b ( )c ( )d

6. In the private sector, individuals try to **(a)** minimize their tax burden **(b)** minimize their individual or private costs **(c)** minimize the amount of time they spend at work **(d)** minimize the costs of government .... ( )a ( )b ( )c ( )d

7. In an exchange of private property in the private sector, **(a)** one party benefits at the cost of another **(b)** both parties to the exchange benefit or the exchange would not take place **(c)** both parties must give up most of the benefit of the exchange **(d)** one party receives the benefits and the other party receives the costs .... ( )a ( )b ( )c ( )d

8. In the economic sense of the word, *efficiency* means **(a)** using a given amount and combination of resources to get the maximum amount of benefit **(b)** raising prices to increase profits **(c)** assigning workers more to do **(d)** using less input to achieve greater output .... ( )a ( )b ( )c ( )d

9. Competition in the private sector tends to make the economic activities in that sector **(a)** more efficient **(b)** more equitable **(c)** more frequent **(d)** more acceptable to government.......... ( )a ( )b ( )c ( )d

10. Competition in the private sector tends to work to the benefit of **(a)** consumers only **(b)** producers only **(c)** government and voters **(d)** consumers and producers .... ( )a ( )b ( )c ( )d

11. In economics, the noun *market* refers to **(a)** a grocery cooperative **(b)** the practice of selling goods for profit **(c)** the exchange activities that take place between buyers and sellers of goods **(d)** a location for the sale of livestock .... ( )a ( )b ( )c ( )d

12. Markets in the private sector provide the following major benefit to consumers: **(a)** price information and substitutes from which the consumer may choose **(b)** a place where the consumers may show the goods that they wish to sell **(c)** an organization that monitors producers to keep them from charging prices that are too high **(d)** an organization that watches consumers to keep them from banding together to drive prices down............. ( )a ( )b ( )c ( )d

13. In the private sector, entrepreneurs **(a)** organize the efforts of a business **(b)** take risks involved in producing a product **(c)** are rewarded with profits when consumers buy the goods they produce and are punished with losses when consumers do not buy their goods **(d)** all of these . . . .   ( )a ( )b ( )c ( )d

14. The private sector, like the public sector, does not function perfectly. One of the pitfalls of the market system in the private sector is that **(a)** sometimes consumers band together and agree not to buy some product and drive the price down unfairly **(b)** there is sometimes a lack of competition in the market by either producers or consumers **(c)** sometimes producers agree to set prices high and not to compete with one another **(d)** all of these. . . . .   ( )a ( )b ( )c ( )d

15. Externalities are **(a)** costs incurred by the consumer in the market **(b)** dollars paid for a product produced in the private sector **(c)** costs such as taxes passed on to the producer of a good or service **(d)** costs such as pollution or crowded parking lots passed on to those outside the market system . . . .   ( )a ( )b ( )c ( )d

16. An example of a positive externality is **(a)** local taxes are raised to support fund-raising by your local library **(b)** restaurant food prices are higher because uneaten food must be discarded **(c)** your property is well lighted by the park lights nearby **(d)** a family of coyotes roams the neighborhood, opening trashbags and threatening outdoor pets . . . .   ( )a ( )b ( )c ( )d

Public Sector Decisions

Part 1 — Building Your Economic Vocabulary

Directions: Complete each of the following sentences with chapter vocabulary from the list below.

> contract
> lobbying
> property rights
> public institutions
> public sector
> special interest group

1. The _____ is that part of the economy that is owned by and operated for the benefit of the whole society.

2. Publicly owned organizations established by government to serve the wants and needs of a whole society are _____.

3. The rules that government has established to define who owns what property and how owners may use their property are _____.

4. A _____ is a legally binding agreement between two or more competent persons.

5. A _____ is an organization of people who are bound together by a common concern.

6. The act of communicating with government representatives to influence their votes on a specific issue is called _____.

Part 2 — Checking Your Economic Knowledge

Directions: Carefully read the following statements. Decide whether the statement is *True* or *False*. Fill in the answer bubble for **T** for *True* or **F** for *False*. If any part of the statement is *False*, then the statement is *False*.

1. The public sector consists of all companies, institutions, and clubs that are operated for a profit. . . . .   ( )T ( )F

2. One valuable function government undertakes in our society is intervening against unfair competition in the private sector. . . . .   ( )T ( )F

3. To keep our markets competitive, the government has established the Federal Trade Commission to police business practices. . . . .   ( )T ( )F

4. One function of the public sector that greatly assists the private sector to function efficiently is the definition and enforcement of property rights. . . . . . .   ( )T ( )F

5. When government establishes and enforces property rights, it improves both equity and efficiency in our economy. . . . .   ( )T ( )F

6. In a modern industrial economy, the need to enforce contracts is unimportant. . . . .   ( )T ( )F

7. The public sector provides some types of goods because the private sector is either unable or unwilling to do so. . . . .   ( )T ( )F

8. The public sector can eliminate all externalities simply by passing laws that make them all illegal. . . . .   ( )T ( )F

9. The public sector tries to improve the equity of our society by redistributing income. . . . .   ( )T ( )F

10. Public goods usually receive more care and maintenance by private citizens than does their own property. . . . .   ( )T ( )F

11. In the public sector, special interest groups are sometimes able to receive personal benefits at a cost passed on to all members of the society. . . . .   ( )T ( )F

12. It is always more efficient to produce goods and services on a large scale than on a small scale. . . . .   ( )T ( )F

Part 3 — Mastering Economic Concepts

Directions: Carefully read the following items. Fill in the answer bubble next to the letter of the *best* answer.

1. The public sector of our economy consists of **(a)** all companies, property, and institutions owned by individuals and operated for their benefit **(b)** bus terminals, stores, shops, and other places that are open to the public **(c)** all levels of government in our economy and the institutions that government establishes to help our economy function **(d)** the offices of public servants such as notary publics, lawyers, and city mayors . . . .   ( )a ( )b ( )c ( )d

2. The public sector attempts to **(a)** provide an environment in which the private sector can function effectively **(b)** establish a court system to define and enforce rights and settle disputes **(c)** create institutions such as the Federal Reserve System and government regulatory agencies to control the system of money **(d)** all of these . . . .   ( )a ( )b ( )c ( )d

3. Which of the following supports strong government to keep corporations in check? **(a)** Clayton **(b)** the FTC **(c)** Galbraith **(d)** Friedman. . . . .   ( )a ( )b ( )c ( )d

4. One of the important contributions of the public sector is that it **(a)** sometimes undertakes activities that the private sector has found to be unprofitable or undesirable **(b)** has always been able to tax the public enough to pay for its public goods **(c)** always finds the cause of air pollution and controls it through the power of law **(d)** has developed great politicians who can control government with great efficiency . . . .   ( )a ( )b ( )c ( )d

5. The existence of competition in a particular industry **(a)** causes firms to advertise and simply drives prices up **(b)** improves the equity in our economy **(c)** improves the efficiency with which our economy operates **(d)** increases the need for government to step in and regulate the industry . . . .   ( )a   ( )b   ( )c   ( )d

6. The Federal Trade Commission is in charge of **(a)** improving U.S. trade with other nations **(b)** enforcing the laws against selling prohibited drugs in the United States **(c)** making laws to prevent businesses from competing **(d)** enforcing laws that keep our markets competitive. . . . .   ( )a   ( )b   ( )c   ( )d

7. The public sector appears to be better suited to doing some types of tasks than is the private sector. One of these tasks is **(a)** acting as a referee to promote competition between businesses **(b)** collecting taxes **(c)** making promises in office **(d)** all of these . . . .   ( )a   ( )b   ( )c   ( )d

8. The private sector functions primarily through the sale or exchange of privately owned goods and services between people and businesses. The public sector assists this exchange process by **(a)** defining the property rights of individuals and corporations **(b)** enforcing the property rights of individuals and corporations **(c)** establishing the legal system to maintain some degree of equity in the economy **(d)** all of these. . . . .   ( )a   ( )b   ( )c   ( )d

9. If the public sector did not enforce contracts between individuals and businesses, **(a)** the production and exchange of goods and services would not be as efficient because neither producers nor consumers could count on each other's promises **(b)** lawyers and judges would earn more than they do now **(c)** the production and exchange of goods and services would be more efficient since there would be less time and money tied up in lawsuits **(d)** there would be no change in the private sector . . . .   ( )a   ( )b   ( )c   ( )d

10. One of the functions that the public sector carries out more efficiently than does the private sector is **(a)** restricting competition **(b)** creating negative externalities **(c)** providing public goods **(d)** defining a market system . . . .   ( )a   ( )b   ( )c   ( )d

11. In many cases, government is best suited to deal with externalities because **(a)** it has the power to make and enforce laws to control externalities **(b)** it has experience in creating negative externalities **(c)** it has the money to pay for damages caused by negative externalities **(d)** all of these. . . . .   ( )a   ( )b   ( )c   ( )d

12. An example of a negative externality might be **(a)** neighbors buying the run-down and abandoned house next to yours and fixing it up **(b)** steel factories in your city polluting the air by burning high-sulfur coal in their furnaces **(c)** both (a) and (b) **(d)** none of these . . . .   ( )a   ( )b   ( )c   ( )d

13. The public sector may be better suited to the task of redistributing income than is the private sector because only government **(a)** has the power to tax **(b)** has more money to give away than the private sector does **(c)** is concerned with lower-income persons **(d)** wants to prevent revolutions . . . .   ( )a ( )b ( )c ( )d

14. The public sector redistributes income primarily to **(a)** make the distribution of goods and services in our economy more efficient **(b)** make the distribution of goods and services in our economy more equitable **(c)** increase the production of goods and services in our economy **(d)** reduce the number of wealthy individuals in our economy. . . . .   ( )a ( )b ( )c ( )d

15. One of the problems with the provision of public goods is that **(a)** people do not care for and maintain public goods as well as they do their own personal property **(b)** public goods are frequently stolen **(c)** public goods are more costly to provide than are private goods **(d)** public goods are used more frequently by high-income individuals than by low-income individuals . . . . . .   ( )a ( )b ( )c ( )d

16. A frequent criticism of the public sector is that it **(a)** is too small to handle its responsibilities **(b)** has become too large to be efficiently controlled **(c)** does not have enough legal power to do its job **(d)** has more power than is necessary to redistribute income . . . .   ( )a ( )b ( )c ( )d

Demand: Achieving Consumer Satisfaction

Part 1 — Building Your Economic Vocabulary

Directions: Match the following terms with the definitions below.

A. complementary products
B. demand
C. demand curve
D. demand schedule
E. determinants of demand
F. diminishing marginal utility
G. income effect
H. inferior goods

I. law of demand
J. marginal utility
K. normal goods
L. price elasticity of demand
M. substitute products
N. substitution effect
O. total revenue

_____ 1. goods for which demand goes down as income goes up

_____ 2. the total amount of money a company receives from sales of a product

_____ 3. a listing of the quantities that would be purchased at various prices

_____ 4. the quantity demanded of a good will be greater at lower prices than will be the quantity demanded at higher prices

_____ 5. goods for which demand goes up as income goes up

_____ 6. the principle that as additional units of a product are consumed during a given time period, the additional satisfaction decreases

_____ 7. the effect that increasing or decreasing prices has on the buying power of income

_____ 8. the change in the mix of goods purchased as a result of increasing or decreasing relative prices

_____ 9. a graphic illustration of the relationship between price and the quantity demanded at each price

_____ 10. the factors that determine how much will be purchased at any given price

_____ 11. the quantities of a good that consumers are willing and able to purchase at various prices during a given period of time

_____ 12. the amount of satisfaction a person gets from *one* additional unit of a product

_____ 13. products that are used together

_____ 14. products whose uses are similar enough that one can replace the other

_____ 15. measures the relative responsiveness of the change in quantity demanded as a result of a change in a product's price

 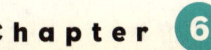

Part 2 — Checking Your Economic Knowledge

Directions: Carefully read the following statements. Decide whether the statement is *True* or *False*. Fill in the answer bubble for **T** for *True* or **F** for *False*. If any part of the statement is *False,* then the statement is *False.*

1. The demand schedule for a good is simply a listing of the various prices at which the good is offered for sale and the quantities demanded at each price.. . ( )T ( )F

2. The demand curve is the graphic illustration of the demand schedule showing the relationship between price and quantity demanded. . . . . ( )T ( )F

3. The concept of diminishing marginal utility means that as you consume more of a product over the years you become less and less satisfied.. . . . . ( )T ( )F

4. The economic concept of an income effect means that as you earn more and more income you can buy more goods. . . . . ( )T ( )F

5. In economics, the substitution effect refers to the fact that as the price of a good falls consumers may substitute that good into their budgets in place of some other good that satisfies almost the same need. . . . . ( )T ( )F

6. If consumers receive higher incomes or change their attitudes more favorably toward a specific good, we would expect that the demand for that good would increase. . . . . ( )T ( )F

7. If the price of margarine increases, then we would expect that the demand for butter would fall. . . . . ( )T ( )F

8. Personal computers and floppy disks are complementary products. . . . . ( )T ( )F

9. If a certain good is price elastic, then consumers will buy about the same amount if the price is increased . . . . ( )T ( )F

10. Just how price elastic a certain good is depends on the number of substitutes available for the product, how important the product is in a person's budget, and the time period it takes to make the product. ( )T ( )F

11. Big-ticket items such as appliances, cars, and houses are likely to have a more inelastic demand . . . . ( )T ( )F

12. Total revenue increases whenever price increases. . . . . ( )T ( )F

Part 3 — Mastering Economic Concepts

Directions: Carefully read the following items. Fill in the answer bubble with the letter of the *best* answer.

1. The main reason individuals consume goods and services is
   (a) to increase personal satisfaction **(b)** increase demand
   (c) both (a) and (b) **(d)** none of these. . . . . ( )a ( )b ( )c ( )d

2. Economists define the concept of demand as **(a)** those things that people simply demand to have **(b)** the quantities of a good that consumers are willing and able to purchase at various prices during a given period of time **(c)** the various prices that consumers are willing to pay for goods over time **(d)** the various times that consumers are willing to pay certain prices for the same quantity of goods . . . . ( )a ( )b ( )c ( )d

3. For demand to be an effective demand, consumers must be **(a)** willing to buy exactly what sellers want to sell **(b)** both willing and able to buy a particular good **(c)** willing to buy all of a particular good that a seller can provide to the market **(d)** able to choose carefully among the various goods in the market . . . .   ( )a ( )b ( )c ( )d

4. On a demand schedule, if the various prices of a good are shown in rising order, we would expect the accompanying value of the quantities demanded to **(a)** also be rising **(b)** be falling as the prices increase **(c)** stay the same as prices rise **(d)** both rise and fall as prices rise . . . .   ( )a ( )b ( )c ( )d

5. If we plot the information that we have in a demand schedule onto a graph with prices on the vertical axis and the quantities demanded on the horizontal axis, we get a **(a)** demand curve **(b)** demand schedule **(c)** demand **(d)** quantity demanded schedule . . . .   ( )a ( )b ( )c ( )d

6. The law of demand is the rule that **(a)** consumers are willing to buy more of a good at lower prices than at higher prices **(b)** consumers are willing to buy more of a good at higher prices than at lower prices **(c)** as prices rise, the quantity of a particular good that consumers will buy also rises **(d)** the more consumers purchase a good, the greater the demand for the good. . . . .   ( )a ( )b ( )c ( )d

7. The concept of diminishing marginal utility means that **(a)** the more of a product that you consume, the less total satisfaction you will get from the product **(b)** as you consume more of a product, your demand for the product will diminish **(c)** increases in marginal utility diminish the amount of a product you can possibly consume **(d)** as you consume more units of a product during a given time period, additional units provide less and less additional satisfaction . . . .   ( )a ( )b ( )c ( )d

8. The income effect happens when **(a)** the price of some product declines, giving you the ability to buy more of that product or any other with the same amount of money **(b)** you receive increases in your income and therefore can buy more of all goods that you consume **(c)** the general price of products changes but your income stays the same **(d)** none of these. . . . .   ( )a ( )b ( )c ( )d

9. An example of the substitution effect is **(a)** the price of home heating oil rising so consumers begin to substitute wood-burning stoves and solar collectors to heat their homes **(b)** individuals finding that butter has too many calories and so substituting margarine in its place **(c)** the price of import cars decreasing, so you purchase a higher priced vehicle than you could have afforded previously **(d)** both (a) and (c). . . . .   ( )a ( )b ( )c ( )d

10. Use the following table for questions 10–13. If the price of a liter of spring water increases from $2 to $4, quantity demanded **(a)** decreases by 10 units **(b)** increases by 20 units **(c)** decreases by 20 units **(d)** increases by 10 units. . . . . ( )a ( )b ( )c ( )d

Demand for Spring Water	
Price	**Quantity Demanded**
$5	10
4	20
3	30
2	40
1	50

11. If the price of a liter of spring water increases from $1 to $5, quantity demanded goes from 50 to 10 units. This is a **(a)** change in demand **(b)** change in quantity demanded **(c)** change in determinants of demand **(d)** change in the entire demand schedule . . . . ( )a ( )b ( )c ( )d

12. If the demand schedule for spring water is graphed, the curve will **(a)** slope downward to the right **(b)** slope upward to the right **(c)** curve up to and down from 30, the middle quantity demanded **(d)** none of these . . . . ( )a ( )b ( )c ( )d

13. If this demand schedule is for spring water in one shop for one week, then total revenue for that week is **(a)** $30 if the shop has a price of $3 **(b)** $90 if the shop has a price of $3 **(c)** $350 **(d)** none of these . . . . ( )a ( )b ( )c ( )d

14. A change in one of the determinants of demand will cause **(a)** the entire demand curve to shift either to the right or to the left **(b)** the demand curve to get shorter **(c)** no change in the demand curve **(d)** a change in the price of the good offered . . . . . ( )a ( )b ( )c ( )d

15. Of the following, the one that is *not* a determinant of demand is **(a)** the amount of income consumers have available to spend **(b)** the attitude that consumers have about a product **(c)** the prices of either substitutes or complementary products **(d)** the quantity of substitutes and complementary products that exist for the good considered. . . . . ( )a ( )b ( )c ( )d

16. When the percentage change in quantity is less than the percentage change in price, the product has **(a)** an elastic demand **(b)** unitary price elasticity **(c)** an inelastic demand **(d)** a calculated value greater than 1 . . . . ( )a ( )b ( )c ( )d

17. Of the following, the one that is *not* a factor in determining the price elasticity of a good is **(a)** the number of substitutes for the good **(b)** the importance of the product in the budget **(c)** the time period considered **(d)** the income level of the buyer. . . . . ( )a ( )b ( )c ( )d

18. If producers increase price and total revenue increases, the producers know that they face a demand curve that is **(a)** price elastic **(b)** income inelastic **(c)** income elastic **(d)** price inelastic. . . . ( )a ( )b ( )c ( )d

Supply: Producing Goods and Services

Part 1 — Building Your Economic Vocabulary

Directions: Complete each of the following sentences with chapter vocabulary from the list below.

average product	factor of production	returns to scale
capital	labor	scale of production
change in supply	land	short run
change in the quantity supplied	law of supply	supply
diminishing marginal product	long run	supply curve
entrepreneurship	marginal product	supply schedule
explicit costs	price elasticity of supply	total product

1. The quantity of a product or service that a firm is willing and able to make available for sale at different prices is _____.

2. A _____ is a table that shows the quantities of a good or service that would be supplied by a firm at different prices.

3. A _____ is a graphic representation of the quantities that would be supplied at each price.

4. The _____ states that the quantity of goods supplied will be greater at a higher price than it will be at a lower price.

5. A change in the number of units made available for sale due to a price change is a _____.

6. _____ measures the responsiveness of the quantity supplied to changes in the product's price.

7. A change in the number of units supplied at every price is a _____.

8. Anything used to produce a good or service is a _____.

9. _____ is a broad measure representing all the basic natural resources that contribute to production.

10. The human factor of production is _____.

11. _____ is previously produced goods used to produce other goods.

12. The managerial ability and risk taking that contribute so much to a productive economy is _____.

13. All the units of a product produced in a given period of time is the _____.

14. The number of units of output produced per unit of input is the _____.

15. The amount that total product increases or decreases as a result of adding one additional unit of input is _____.

16. The _____ is any period during which the usable amount of at least one input is fixed while the usable amount of at least one other input can change.

17. _____ is the principle that as more of an input is added to a fixed amount of other inputs, the marginal product decreases.

18. A period during which the amounts of all inputs can be changed is the _____.

19. The overall level of use of all factors of production is the _____.

20. The relationship between changes in the scale of production and the corresponding change in the amount of output is the _____.

21. Payments made to others as a cost of running a business are the _____.

Part 2 — Checking Your Economic Knowledge

Directions: Carefully read the following statements. Decide whether the statement is *True* or *False*. Fill in the answer bubble for **T** for *True* or **F** for *False*. If any part of the statement is *False,* then the statement is *False.*

1. In general, production takes place because individuals hope to receive personal benefits from their efforts to produce.. ( )T ( )F

2. A supply schedule is a table of the different prices at which a good or service may be offered for sale and the quantities that producers are willing and able to supply.. ( )T ( )F

3. The supply curve is the graphical picture of the supply schedule showing the relationship between price and the quantity demanded. .... ( )T ( )F

4. The law of supply states that the quantity of goods supplied will be less at a higher price than it will at a lower price............................... ( )T ( )F

5. Capital includes all the natural resources and people that contribute to production. .... ( )T ( )F

6. In measuring production we usually count units rather than dollar sales or dollar value of output because units allow us to more accurately compare what is produced from one time period to the next......................... ( )T ( )F

7. Average product is total output divided by the number of units of input used... ( )T ( )F

8. Marginal product is the amount that total product increases or decreases resulting from the addition of one more unit of an input. .... ( )T ( )F

9. If you built a new assembly plant that was twice as large as your old one and it enabled you to more than double your output, you would have realized decreasing returns to scale....................................... ( )T ( )F

10. An accurate estimate of production costs from an economist's point of view includes only explicit costs. .... ( )T ( )F

Part 3 — Mastering Economic Concepts

Directions: Carefully read the following items. Fill in the answer bubble next to the letter of the *best* answer.

1. An increase in supply can be graphed as **(a)** a shift of the supply curve outward and to the right **(b)** a shift of the supply curve inward and to the left **(c)** a movement along the supply curve from one price level to another **(d)** none of these . . . .   ( )a ( )b ( )c ( )d

2. If only the price of a specific good or service changes, we know that there has been **(a)** only a change in the quantity supplied **(b)** a change in the supply curve itself **(c)** both a change in supply and in quantity supplied **(d)** no change at all . . . .   ( )a ( )b ( )c ( )d

3. When there is a change in the price of an item, the supply curve shows us that the relationship between the price and the quantity supplied is **(a)** a direct relationship (quantity increases when price increases) **(b)** an indirect relationship (quantity does not change when price changes) **(c)** an inverse relationship (quantity decreases when price increases) **(d)** a diverse relationship (sometimes quantity increases and sometimes it decreases with an increase in price) . . . .   ( )a ( )b ( )c ( )d

4. The price elasticity of supply measures **(a)** the responsiveness of quantity demanded to a change in market price **(b)** how market price changes in regard to a change in supply **(c)** the responsiveness of quantity supplied to a change in price **(d)** how far supply can be stretched to fulfill demand . . . .   ( )a ( )b ( )c ( )d

5. If there is a change in technology or a change in the cost of inputs, we would expect **(a)** only a change in quantity supplied **(b)** a change in supply **(c)** a change in quantity supplied at every price level **(d)** both (b) and (c) . . . .   ( )a ( )b ( )c ( )d

6. The four factors of production are **(a)** metals, building materials, workers, and technical know-how **(b)** land, technology, energy, and resources **(c)** land, labor, capital, and entrepreneurship **(d)** capital, marketing ability, materials, and know-how . . . .   ( )a ( )b ( )c ( )d

7. Natural resources used in the production process, such as iron ore or timber, would be included as a factor of production under the category of **(a)** materials and labor **(b)** land **(c)** capital and marketing **(d)** rent . . . .   ( )a ( )b ( )c ( )d

8. If we measure production in dollar value of what is produced rather than in units, we can sometimes get an incorrect picture of both sales and production because **(a)** price increases can hide the fact that production actually dropped **(b)** production increases can hide the fact that prices actually dropped **(c)** increases in production accompanied by price increases can overstate the real increase in production **(d)** all of these . . . .   ( )a ( )b ( )c ( )d

9. Marginal product measures the amount by which **(a)** average product increases when we use one less unit of input **(b)** total product increases or decreases when we add one more unit of input **(c)** total product increases when we use one less unit of input **(d)** all of these. . . . .   ( )a ( )b ( )c ( )d

10. You have one large flower pot, some seeds, and some fertilizer. If you plant one seed you may get one plant and perhaps two ears of corn. When you add the second seed you may get one more plant and two more ears of corn. As you add more and more seeds, however, you will not continue to get more and more ears of corn because the plants will crowd each other out in the flower pot. In economics, this is an example of **(a)** the law of demand **(b)** the law of supply **(c)** diminishing marginal product **(d)** diminishing marginal utility . . . .   ( )a ( )b ( )c ( )d

11. In the short run, as additional units of input are used, **(a)** output increases less and less rapidly **(b)** the amount of total output decreases steadily **(c)** diminishing marginal product is eliminated **(d)** none of these . . . .   ( )a ( )b ( )c ( )d

12. The long run in economic terminology is that period of time in which the usable amount of **(a)** all inputs in the productive process is variable **(b)** all inputs in the productive process is fixed **(c)** some inputs is fixed while for others it is variable **(d)** none of these. . . . .   ( )a ( )b ( )c ( )d

13. If goods such as automobiles were not produced on a large scale, their price would be much higher because **(a)** this production process benefits from increasing returns to scale **(b)** decreasing returns to scale exist in this production process **(c)** output of these goods increases more rapidly than the rate of increase in the use of inputs **(d)** both (a) and (c) . . . .   ( )a ( )b ( )c ( )d

14. When the rate of increase in output is the same as the rate of increase in the inputs used in production, this production process is characterized by **(a)** increasing returns to scale **(b)** decreasing returns to scale **(c)** diminishing marginal productivity **(d)** constant returns to scale. . . . .   ( )a ( )b ( )c ( )d

15. The payments for the four factors of production are **(a)** land, labor, capital, and entrepreneurship **(b)** rent, wages, interest, and profit **(c)** explicit costs, opportunity costs, returns to scale, and scale of production **(d)** none of these. . . . .   ( )a ( )b ( )c ( )d

16. An example of an opportunity cost that a business might encounter in its operation is **(a)** the forgone rental income that it would receive if it rented out its building **(b)** the forgone alternative salary its owners would have earned in other jobs **(c)** the forgone interest that the owners would have earned on their savings if they had not invested those savings in the business **(d)** all of these . . . .   ( )a ( )b ( )c ( )d

17. As businesses enter the long run and change the scale of production, the cost of producing each unit could **(a)** increase **(b)** decrease **(c)** stay the same **(d)** all of these . . . .   ( )a ( )b ( )c ( )d

Demand, Supply, and Prices

Part 1 — Building Your Economic Vocabulary

Directions: Complete each of the following sentences with chapter vocabulary from the list below.

> equilibrium price
> equilibrium quantity
> price ceiling
> price floor
> shortage
> surplus

1. _____ is the price at which the quantity demanded equals the quantity supplied.

2. _____ is the quantity that is both demanded and supplied at the equilibrium price.

3. A _____ occurs when demand is greater than supply at a certain price.

4. When supply is greater than demand at a certain price, a _____ results.

5. A minimum price set by government that is above the market equilibrium price is a _____.

6. A _____ is a maximum price set by government that is below the market equilibrium price.

Part 2 — Checking Your Economic Knowledge

Directions: Carefully read the following statements. Decide whether the statement is *True* or *False*. Fill in the answer bubble for **T** for *True* or **F** for *False*. If any part of the statement is *False*, then the statement is *False*.

1. In a market economy, natural economic forces lead to an equilibrium between demand and supply. . . . .   ( )T ( )F

2. If demand increases with no change in supply, equilibrium price will rise and equilibrium quantity will fall. . . . .   ( )T ( )F

3. If supply increases with no change in demand, equilibrium price and equilibrium quantity will fall. . . . .   ( )T ( )F

4. Price changes help eliminate shortages and surpluses.. . . . .   ( )T ( )F

5. If quantity demanded exceeds quantity supplied, price will rise, and only those consumers willing and able to pay the increased prices will get the available goods. . . . .   ( )T ( )F

 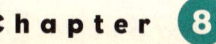

6. If quantity supplied exceeds quantity demanded, producers will compete for the available consumers by lowering price, and only those producers willing and able to provide their goods at each lower price will be able to sell their goods. .   ( )T ( )F

7. If government imposes a price floor above the natural market equilibrium, quantity demanded will be less than quantity supplied at that price. . . . .   ( )T ( )F

8. If government imposes a price floor below the market equilibrium price, it will have no effect on the market equilibrium price and quantity. . . . .   ( )T ( )F

9. If government imposes a price ceiling below the market equilibrium price, quantity demanded will be less than quantity supplied at that price. . . . .   ( )T ( )F

10. When government sets a price ceiling, a surplus usually results. . . . .   ( )T ( )F

Part 3 — Mastering Economic Concepts

Directions: Carefully read the following items. Fill in the answer bubble next to the letter of the *best* answer. Use the following table for questions 1–4.

Demand and Supply: Pumpkin Pie		
Price	Quantity Demanded	Quantity Supplied
$2.80	2,400	1,600
3.00	2,300	1,700
3.20	2,200	1,800
3.40	2,100	2,000
3.60	2,000	2,000
3.80	1,900	2,100
4.00	1,800	2,200
4.20	1,700	2,300
4.40	1,600	2,400

1. The equilibrium price level for pumpkin pies is **(a)** $4.40 **(b)** $2.80 **(c)** $3.60 **(d)** $3.80 . . . .   ( )a ( )b ( )c ( )d

2. At a market price of $4.00, there would be **(a)** a shortage of 400 pumpkin pies **(b)** a surplus of 200 pumpkin pies **(c)** a surplus of 400 pumpkin pies **(d)** market equilibrium . . . .   ( )a ( )b ( )c ( )d

3. If government established a price floor of $3.80, we would expect **(a)** a surplus of 200 pumpkin pies **(b)** suppliers to supply more than the equilibrium quantity **(c)** consumers to demand less than the equilibrium quantity **(d)** all of these . . . .   ( )a ( )b ( )c ( )d

4. If government established a price ceiling of $3.40, we would expect the market to **(a)** have a shortage of 100 pumpkin pies **(b)** have a surplus of 200 pumpkin pies **(c)** attain equilibrium by itself **(d)** have a shortage of 600 pumpkin pies . . . .   ( )a ( )b ( )c ( )d

5. The equilibrium price in a market is the price level at which **(a)** the supply curve parallels the demand curve **(b)** the supply curve intersects the demand curve **(c)** the demand curve reaches the price ceiling **(d)** none of these . . . .   ( )a ( )b ( )c ( )d

6. A market is in equilibrium when **(a)** the quantity demanded is greater than quantity supplied **(b)** the quantity supplied is greater than the quantity demanded **(c)** the quantity demanded equals the quantity supplied **(d)** none of these . . . .   ( )a ( )b ( )c ( )d

7. In a market system, price functions as **(a)** a means of adjusting the balance between the forces of supply and demand **(b)** a means of rationing the available supply among those who would demand it **(c)** an incentive to producers to either increase or decrease the quantity supplied **(d)** all of these . . . .   ( )a ( )b ( )c ( )d

8. When economists refer to a shortage, they are referring to **(a)** the amount by which quantity demanded exceeds quantity supplied at the present market price **(b)** the amount by which quantity supplied exceeds quantity demanded at the present market price **(c)** the fact that producers are supplying more than consumers are willing to buy **(d)** none of these. . . . .   ( )a ( )b ( )c ( )d

9. A shortage exists when quantity demanded at a certain price is **(a)** greater than quantity supplied and there is upward pressure on price **(b)** less than quantity supplied and there is a downward pressure on price **(c)** equal to quantity supplied and there is no pressure for change on price **(d)** none of these. . . . .   ( )a ( )b ( )c ( )d

10. In economic terminology, a surplus is **(a)** the amount by which quantity demanded exceeds quantity supplied at a certain price **(b)** the result when quantity demanded and supplied are equal at a certain price **(c)** the amount by which quantity supplied exceeds quantity demanded at a certain price **(d)** a situation in which there are leftover goods from a specific activity such as a U.S. Army surplus . . . .   ( )a ( )b ( )c ( )d

11. In a market functioning without restrictions, if a surplus exists, we would expect **(a)** quantity demanded to rise and quantity supplied to fall as the market price rises **(b)** quantity supplied to fall and quantity demanded to rise as the market price falls **(c)** supply to increase and demand to fall as price changes **(d)** none of these . . . .   ( )a ( )b ( )c ( )d

12. Which is NOT one of the primary factors that can cause a change in demand? **(a)** consumers' incomes may change **(b)** producers' attitudes or expectations may change **(c)** the prices of substitute products may change **(d)** the prices of complementary products may change . . . .   ( )a ( )b ( )c ( )d

13. If a market is in equilibrium and then consumers' incomes increase, other things held constant, economists would predict that **(a)** demand would increase **(b)** market price would rise **(c)** the quantity exchanged in the marketplace would rise **(d)** all of these. . . . .   ( )a ( )b ( )c ( )d

14. If the supply curve stays the same and demand increases, **(a)** the quantity exchanged will fall **(b)** the market price will fall **(c)** both (a) and (b) **(d)** none of these . . . .   ( )a ( )b ( )c ( )d

15. If the market for butter is in equilibrium and the price of margarine then rises and other things hold constant, we would expect **(a)** the demand for butter to rise **(b)** the quantity of butter exchanged in the market to rise **(c)** the price of butter to rise **(d)** all of these . . . .   ( )a   ( )b   ( )c   ( )d

16. If supply increases while the demand curve remains the same, **(a)** the market price will fall **(b)** the quantity exchanged will rise **(c)** both (a) and (b) **(d)** none of these. . . . .   ( )a   ( )b   ( )c   ( )d

17. When there is a market surplus, **(a)** the existing market price is below the market equilibrium price **(b)** the existing market price is above the market equilibrium price **(c)** the existing market price and the market equilibrium price are equal **(d)** there is no downward pressure on market price . . . .   ( )a   ( )b   ( )c   ( )d

18. In a market system that functions without restrictions, if the present market price is below the equilibrium price, we would expect **(a)** market price to rise **(b)** quantity demanded to decrease **(c)** quantity supplied to increase **(d)** all of these . . . .   ( )a   ( )b   ( )c   ( )d

Business Firms in the Economy

Part 1 — Building Your Economic Vocabulary

Directions: Match the following terms with the definitions below.

A. articles of incorporation
B. bond
C. charter
D. common stock
E. conglomerate
F. conglomerate merger
G. corporation
H. dividends
I. franchise
J. horizontal merger
K. interest
L. limited liability

M. line of credit
N. merger
O. multinational business
P. nonprofit organization
Q. partnership
R. partnership agreement
S. proprietorship
T. stock
U. test of the market
V. unlimited liability
W. vertical merger

_____ **1.** a form of business in which there is one owner

_____ **2.** the concept that an owner's personal assets can be used to pay bills of the business

_____ **3.** a type of business organization in which there are two or more owners

_____ **4.** a legally binding document that specifies how the responsibilities and profits or losses from a partnership will be split between the partners

_____ **5.** an organization of people legally bound together by a charter to conduct some type of business

_____ **6.** a written application of the state requesting permission to form a corporation

_____ **7.** the legal authorization to organize a business as a corporation

_____ **8.** shares of ownership in a corporation

_____ **9.** the concept that owners of a business are only responsible for its debts up to the amount they invest in the business

_____ **10.** part of a corporation's income paid to its stockholders

_____ **11.** being able to provide goods that satisfy consumers' needs and desires at prices consumers are willing to pay

_____ **12.** a firm that sells and produces products in multiple countries

 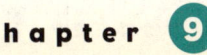

_____ **13.** an organization that does not have profit as its objective

_____ **14.** a contract between a parent company and some other business or individual that details the terms under which the franchisee does business with products, names, or other services of the franchisor

_____ **15.** an arrangement through which a business can access needed cash from a bank quickly

_____ **16.** a certificate stating the amount the corporation has borrowed from the holder and the terms of repayment

_____ **17.** the payment for using someone else's money

_____ **18.** a type of stock that gives the holder a partial ownership of the corporation

_____ **19.** the combining of one company with another company it buys

_____ **20.** a merger of two companies in the same industry

_____ **21.** a merger of two companies that are at different stages of the production process in the same industry

_____ **22.** a merger of two companies that are in different businesses

_____ **23.** a firm made up of many divisions and/or subsidiaries that may not have much in common in their lines of business

Part 2 — Checking Your Economic Knowledge

Directions: Carefully read the following statements. Decide whether the statement is _True_ or _False._ Fill in the answer bubble for **T** for _True_ or **F** for _False._ If any part of the statement is _False,_ then the statement is _False._

1. The three major forms of business organization in the United States are proprietorships, partnerships, and mergers. . . . .   ( )T ( )F

2. A proprietorship is a business that is owned and operated by a single individual and that pays taxes on its income before the owner receives any income. . . . . . .   ( )T ( )F

3. A proprietorship ceases to exist as a business at the death of the proprietor. . . . .   ( )T ( )F

4. Two advantages of the corporate form of business organization are limited liability and unlimited life. . . . .   ( )T ( )F

5. There are more corporations in the United States than there are any of the other forms of business organization. . . . .   ( )T ( )F

6. Most of the dollars of sales in the United States are earned by proprietorships. .   ( )T ( )F

7. Some corporations have annual sales revenues that are larger than the total output of many countries in the world. . . . .   ( )T ( )F

8. If General Motors (a car manufacturer) merged with your local car dealer, this
   would be a horizontal merger. . . . .   ( )T ( )F

9. If Bob's record store and Mary's shoe store merged into one corporate business,
   this would be a vertical merger. . . . .   ( )T ( )F

10. If Spaulding Sporting Goods merged with International Health Spas and Hertz
    Rent-a-Car, this would be a conglomerate merger. . . . .   ( )T ( )F

Part 3 — Mastering Economic Concepts

Directions: Carefully read the following items. Fill in the answer bubble next to the letter of the
best answer.

1. A form of business organization that is privately owned by a
   single individual is classified as **(a)** a corporation **(b)** a partnership
   (c) a proprietorship **(d)** none of these . . . .   ( )a ( )b ( )c ( )d

2. Of the following, the one that is NOT an advantage of the
   proprietorship form of business organization is **(a)** it is easy to
   start and there is little government control **(b)** the owner has
   complete control and enjoys pride of ownership **(c)** all the profits
   go to the owner **(d)** there is unlimited liability for the owner . . . .   ( )a ( )b ( )c ( )d

3. Partnerships are businesses in which **(a)** all partners are responsible for the debts and other liabilities of the business **(b)** two
   or more persons join together to form the business **(c)** both
   (a) and (b) **(d)** partners are responsible for the debts of the
   business in proportion to their initial investment in the business. .   ( )a ( )b ( )c ( )d

4. Of the following, the one that is a disadvantage of partnerships
   is **(a)** they are difficult to start and are subject to much
   government regulation **(b)** they can raise large amounts of
   capital **(c)** the business ceases to exist when one partner dies
   (d) all of these . . . .   ( )a ( )b ( )c ( )d

5. The document that a corporation files that indicates the name,
   address, and type of business of the corporation is **(a)** the
   corporate charter **(b)** the articles of confederation **(c)** the articles
   of incorporation **(d)** the preamble to the corporate constitution . .   ( )a ( )b ( )c ( )d

6. Corporations are business organizations that **(a)** have a legal
   identity separate from their owners **(b)** involve people legally
   bound together by a charter to conduct some specific type of
   business **(c)** limit the liability of their owners to the amount of
   the owners' original investment in the stock of the company
   (d) all of these . . . .   ( )a ( )b ( )c ( )d

7. An important advantage of the corporate form of business
   organization is **(a)** the limited liability of stockholders **(b)** the
   ability to raise large amounts of financial capital **(c)** the fact
   that the business lives on even if the owners of the business die
   (d) all of these . . . .   ( )a ( )b ( )c ( )d

8. In a corporation **(a)** the risks of a business loss are spread over many stockholders **(b)** management of the business is usually much more specialized than in proprietorships or partnerships **(c)** dividends are paid to its stockholders **(d)** all of these . . . .   ( )a ( )b ( )c ( )d

9. The only form of business organization subject to double taxation is the **(a)** corporation **(b)** partnership **(c)** proprietorship **(d)** none of these . . . .   ( )a ( )b ( )c ( )d

10. Most of the goods and services produced in our economy are produced by **(a)** government **(b)** nonprofit charitable organizations **(c)** private businesses, generally for profit **(d)** individual professionals such as lawyers and doctors . . . .   ( )a ( )b ( )c ( )d

11. Most businesses are organized as **(a)** partnerships **(b)** proprietorships **(c)** corporations **(d)** none of these . . . .   ( )a ( )b ( )c ( )d

12. The form of business organization that does most of the dollar volume of sales in our economy is **(a)** the corporation **(b)** the proprietorship **(c)** the partnership **(d)** the nonprofit charitable proprietorship. . . . .   ( )a ( )b ( )c ( )d

13. A type of franchise is **(a)** a retail franchise granted by a manufacturer **(b)** a wholesale franchise granted by a manufacturer **(c)** a service-sponsored retailer **(d)** all of these . . . . .   ( )a ( )b ( )c ( )d

14. The most frequently used means of financing a corporation include all of the following except **(a)** issuing corporate stock **(b)** issuing corporate bonds **(c)** borrowing from banks **(d)** asking stockholders for additional investments . . . .   ( )a ( )b ( )c ( )d

15. If you bought a bond from a corporation, you would be **(a)** a creditor of the corporation (you would have loaned them your money to be repaid with interest) **(b)** an owner of the corporation **(c)** both an owner and a creditor of the corporation **(d)** none of these . . . .   ( )a ( )b ( )c ( )d

16. If you bought the common stock of a corporation, **(a)** you would be a part owner of the corporation **(b)** the corporation would pay you a guaranteed interest rate on the shares of stock you owned **(c)** you could earn profits from the sale of your stock if the market price of the stock went higher than the price that you paid **(d)** both (a) and (c) . . . .   ( )a ( )b ( )c ( )d

17. When one business buys another business at the same level in the manufacturing or service production process, it is called **(a)** a horizontal merger **(b)** a vertical merger **(c)** a joint revenue **(d)** a corporate buyout . . . .   ( )a ( )b ( )c ( )d

18. When two businesses that are at two different levels in the same production process combine to form a single firm, this action is referred to as **(a)** a horizontal merger **(b)** a corporate bailout **(c)** a vertical merger **(d)** all of these . . . .   ( )a ( )b ( )c ( )d

19. Conglomerates are formed when two or more firms **(a)** in the same industry combine to form a single firm **(b)** in completely separate industries combine to form a single firm **(c)** split off to start separate businesses in different industries **(d)** split off to start businesses in the same industry . . . .   ( )a ( )b ( )c ( )d

Perfect Competition and Monopoly

Part 1 — Building Your Economic Vocabulary

Directions: Match the following terms with the definitions below.

A. economic profit
B. homogeneous product
C. market organization
D. monopoly
E. natural monopoly

F. patent
G. perfect competition
H. price setter
I. price taker

_____ **1.** the way participants in markets are organized and how many participants there are

_____ **2.** a firm that takes a price determined by forces outside the firm's control

_____ **3.** a firm that has some control over the price at which its product sells

_____ **4.** a form of market organization in which a great many small firms produce a homogeneous product

_____ **5.** a good or service that varies little from producer to producer

_____ **6.** total revenue minus total costs

_____ **7.** a form of market organization in which there is only one seller of a product

_____ **8.** a situation in which it is not practical to have competition

_____ **9.** a legal protection for the inventor of a product or process that gives that person or company the sole right to produce the product or use the process for up to 17 years

Part 2 — Checking Your Economic Knowledge

Directions: Carefully read the following statements. Decide whether the statement is *True* or *False*. Fill in the answer bubble for **T** for *True* or **F** for *False*. If any part of the statement is *False,* then the statement is *False.*

1. The four major market organizations are characterized by the number of firms in a market, the type of product sold, the ease of entering and leaving the industry, the amount of information about the market, and the degree of price control. . . . . ( )T ( )F

2. One characteristic of perfectly competitive markets is that the products of the firms are so similar that producers use brand names so consumers can tell the products apart. . . . . ( )T ( )F

3. Perfect competitors usually have perfect or nearly perfect information about the market. . . . .   ( )T ( )F

4. In perfect competition, there are many firms, but they have no control over price. . . . .   ( )T ( )F

5. The demand curve for a firm in perfect competition is a horizontal line. . . . .   ( )T ( )F

6. In perfect competition, firms make no income. . . . .   ( )T ( )F

7. It is usually very difficult to enter a market that is a monopoly. . . . .   ( )T ( )F

8. In a monopoly, there is only one producer, and the producer has complete price control and will always make large profits. . . . .   ( )T ( )F

9. Because monopolists always have complete control over price, there is no limit to the amount of economic profit they can make.. . . . .   ( )T ( )F

10. The demand curve for a monopoly is a vertical line. . . . .   ( )T ( )F

Part 3 — Mastering Economic Concepts

Directions: Carefully read the following items. Fill in the answer bubble next to the letter of the *best* answer.

1. Of the following, the one that is NOT a form of market organization is **(a)** perfect competition **(b)** monopoly **(c)** imperfect competition **(d)** oligopoly. . . . .   ( )a ( )b ( )c ( )d

2. The characteristics economists use to analyze the different kinds of market organization include all of the following except the **(a)** number of firms in the market **(b)** ease of entering or leaving the market **(c)** size of the firms in the market **(d)** kind of product sold . . . .   ( )a ( )b ( )c ( )d

3. Perfectly competitive firms are ones that exist in a market in which **(a)** many sellers sell nearly identical products **(b)** many sellers sell different products **(c)** a few sellers sell nearly identical products **(d)** a few sellers sell different products. . . . .   ( )a ( )b ( )c ( )d

4. Of the following, the one that is a homogeneous product is **(a)** Apple computers **(b)** Iowa wheat **(c)** Crest toothpaste **(d)** Gold Medal flour. . . . .   ( )a ( )b ( )c ( )d

5. In perfect competition, **(a)** all buyers and sellers have perfect information about prices and costs of inputs **(b)** firms can easily enter or leave the market **(c)** no single buyer or seller is a large enough part of the total market to have any effect on price **(d)** all of these . . . .   ( )a ( )b ( )c ( )d

6. Of the following, the one that is NOT a characteristic of perfect competition is **(a)** there are so many producers that each is a small percentage of the market **(b)** the product is homogeneous **(c)** there is not very good information about the market **(d)** it is relatively easy to enter the market . . . .   ( )a ( )b ( )c ( )d

7. Price takers are firms in **(a)** perfectly competitive markets **(b)** monopolistic markets **(c)** oligopolistic markets **(d)** imperfect markets. . . . .   ( )a ( )b ( )c ( )d

8. In perfect competition, a firm's demand curve is **(a)** a downward sloping line **(b)** a vertical line **(c)** an upward sloping line **(d)** a horizontal line . . . . ( )a ( )b ( )c ( )d

9. In perfect competition, if the market price of the product is $4.00, **(a)** you will be better off if you sell yours for $3.90 **(b)** you can sell all you produce at the market price **(c)** you can find some buyers if you sell at $4.10 **(d)** none of these . . . . ( )a ( )b ( )c ( )d

10. Since firms in perfect competition will be led to produce an amount of output at which economic profit is zero, **(a)** owners will not make a good living **(b)** owners' income is not part of economic profit, so owners will still make a living **(c)** there is no excess return **(d)** both (b) and (c) . . . . ( )a ( )b ( )c ( )d

11. In the long run, perfectly competitive firms earn **(a)** no profits, since new firms will enter the market and drive the price down to the level of unit costs of production **(b)** no excess profits, since there is freedom to enter and leave the market **(c)** some excess profits, since firms are only in business to produce profits **(d)** economic losses, since new firms drive the price down below the costs of production . . . . ( )a ( )b ( )c ( )d

12. In perfect competition, the market demand curve is **(a)** a downward-sloping line **(b)** a vertical line **(c)** an upward-sloping line **(d)** a horizontal line. . . . . ( )a ( )b ( )c ( )d

13. From the point of view of the whole economy, perfect competition is desirable because in the long run **(a)** production is as efficient as possible **(b)** price equals the additional cost of producing one more unit of output **(c)** no excess profits exist **(d)** all of these . . . . ( )a ( )b ( )c ( )d

14. In a market characterized as a monopoly, **(a)** there are only a few sellers of a particular product **(b)** the product sold is unique to the monopolist **(c)** both (a) and (b) **(d)** none of these . . . . ( )a ( )b ( )c ( )d

15. The market organization in which entering and leaving the industry is, for all practical purposes, impossible is **(a)** imperfect competition **(b)** perfect competition **(c)** monopoly **(d)** none of these. . . . . ( )a ( )b ( )c ( )d

16. An example of a natural monopoly is **(a)** a company that makes pretzels **(b)** your local electric company **(c)** your barber **(d)** a Midwestern farm . . . . ( )a ( )b ( )c ( )d

17. The purpose of a patent is to **(a)** understand competitors' marketing strategies **(b)** prevent competition for a certain period of time **(c)** enter and leave an industry more easily **(d)** none of these. . . . . ( )a ( )b ( )c ( )d

18. Of the following, the one that is NOT a characteristic of a monopoly is **(a)** the product is unique **(b)** there is very little control over price **(c)** it is difficult to enter or leave the industry **(d)** there isa single producer . . . . ( )a ( )b ( )c ( )d

19. In a monopoly, the firm's demand curve is **(a)** a downward-sloping line **(b)** a vertical line **(c)** an upward-sloping line **(d)** a horizontal line . . . .   ( )a ( )b ( )c ( )d

20. In a monopoly, the firm's demand curve and the market curve are **(a)** the same **(b)** upward sloping **(c)** sloped in opposite directions **(d)** none of these . . . .   ( )a ( )b ( )c ( )d

Monopolistic Competition and Oligopoly

Part 1 — Building Your Economic Vocabulary

Directions: Complete each of the following sentences with chapter vocabulary from the list below.

cartel
collusion
differentiated oligopoly
monopolistic competition
oligopoly
product differentiation
pure oligopoly

1. A market organization in which many firms produce goods that are different but similar enough to be substitutes is _____.

2. The concept that the product of one firm can be distinguished from the products of other firms is known as _____.

3. A form of market organization in which there are relatively few firms is called an _____.

4. An oligopoly in which the products are the same for all firms is a _____.

5. An oligopoly in which the product is differentiated is a _____.

6. _____ is the situation of firms acting together rather than separately.

7. A formal organization of firms in the same industry acting together to make decisions is a _____.

Part 2 — Checking Your Economic Knowledge

Directions: Carefully read the following statements. Decide whether the statement is *True* or *False*. Fill in the answer bubble for **T** for *True* or **F** for *False*. If any part of the statement is *False,* then the statement is *False.*

1. In monopolistic competition, there are very few firms selling products that are very similar but that are viewed as being different by consumers. . . . . ( )T ( )F

2. It is usually very difficult to enter or leave monopolistically competitive industries. . . . . ( )T ( )F

3. The demand curve for an individual firm in monopolistic competition is steeper than the market demand curve. . . . . ( )T ( )F

4. In monopolistic competition, firms have more control over market price than do perfect competitors but less than do monopolies. ( )T ( )F

5. The four major kinds of market organization in the United States are perfect competition, monopoly, oligopoly, and monopolistic competition. . . . .   ( )T ( )F

6. An oligopoly is a firm in a market with many other competitors that has some control over price and can enter or leave the market easily. . . . .   ( )T ( )F

7. Consumers of products produced by an oligopolistic industry are not strongly brand loyal and therefore are good candidates for first-time sales of a new product. . . . .   ( )T ( )F

8. When firms in an industry form a cartel, they are trying to get oligopoly power.   ( )T ( )F

9. An individual oligopolist often faces a demand curve with a kink in it somewhere. . . . .   ( )T ( )F

10. The oligopolist's demand curve has a kink because the competitors are likely to follow a price decrease but not a price increase. . . . .   ( )T ( )F

Part 3 — Mastering Economic Concepts

Directions: Carefully read the following items. Fill in the answer bubble next to the letter of the *best* answer.

1. In monopolistic competition, products are **(a)** homogeneous **(b)** close substitutes **(c)** complementary **(d)** none of these. . . . .   ( )a ( )b ( )c ( )d

2. Of the following products, the one that most consumers would not consider differentiated is **(a)** Crest toothpaste **(b)** Saint Joseph's baby aspirin **(c)** Iowa corn **(d)** Chevrolet Corvette . . . .   ( )a ( )b ( )c ( )d

3. Monopolistic competition is a market structure in which all of the following characteristics exist *except* **(a)** much product differentiation and some price control **(b)** many firms producing products for the market **(c)** no freedom for firms to enter or leave the market **(d)** reasonably complete market information . . .   ( )a ( )b ( )c ( )d

4. There is not very much government regulation in **(a)** an oligopoly **(b)** monopolistic competition **(c)** monopolies **(d)** none of these . . .   ( )a ( )b ( )c ( )d

5. If a single firm in a monopolistically competitive market lowers its price, we expect that **(a)** quantity demanded for that firm's product will increase **(b)** quantity demanded for that firm's product will decrease **(c)** quantity demanded for that firm's product will not change **(d)** none of these . . . .   ( )a ( )b ( )c ( )d

6. The demand curve for an individual firm in monopolistic competition is **(a)** the same as the market demand curve **(b)** a horizontal line **(c)** steeper than the market demand curve **(d)** not as steep as the market demand curve . . . .   ( )a ( )b ( )c ( )d

7. In the long run, the equilibrium price of a product produced in a monopolistically competitive industry will **(a)** be high enough to be profitable for most firms **(b)** be close to the per-unit cost of production **(c)** be so low there will be little incentive for firms to enter the market **(d)** fluctuate depending on other factors . . . . . .   ( )a ( )b ( )c ( )d

8. If the same product could be produced in both a monopolistically competitive market and a perfectly competitive market, we would expect that **(a)** output would be higher in the perfectly competitive market **(b)** price would be lower in the monopolistically competitive market **(c)** price would be lower in the perfectly competitive market **(d)** both (a) and (c) . . . .   ( )a ( )b ( )c ( )d

9. Oligopoly is a market structure in which **(a)** there are few producers **(b)** producers make pricing and output decisions based upon how they think their competitors will react **(c)** it is difficult to enter or leave the market **(d)** all of these . . . .   ( )a ( )b ( )c ( )d

10. An example of a pure oligopoly would be **(a)** agriculture **(b)** utility companies **(c)** the aluminum industry **(d)** the auto industry. . . . .   ( )a ( )b ( )c ( )d

11. The automobile manufacturing industry would be classified as **(a)** a monopoly **(b)** a cartel **(c)** an oligopoly **(d)** monopolistically competitive. . . . .   ( )a ( )b ( )c ( )d

12. Oligopoly is a market structure in which all of the following characteristics exist *except* **(a)** there are either nearly identical or differentiated products **(b)** there are only a few firms **(c)** it is relatively easy to enter or leave the industry **(d)** there is incomplete information about the market . . . .   ( )a ( )b ( )c ( )d

13. Oligopoly is a market structure in which **(a)** there is relatively complete market information **(b)** there is less complete information about the market than in any other form of market organization **(c)** there is more market information than in monopolistic competition **(d)** none of these . . . .   ( )a ( )b ( )c ( )d

14. The market structure that has the greatest amount of control over price is **(a)** a differentiated oligopoly **(b)** a pure oligopoly **(c)** monopolistic competition **(d)** a monopoly . . . .   ( )a ( )b ( )c ( )d

15. Collusion occurs when two or more firms **(a)** act separately to increase competition in a market **(b)** act together to determine price, output, or other important decisions in a market **(c)** are forced by law to charge prices below the market equilibrium price **(d)** charge a price just equal to the additional cost of producing the last unit. . . . .   ( )a ( )b ( )c ( )d

16. A group of firms that agree formally to act together in the market to earn monopoly-type profits is called a **(a)** price leader **(b)** monopoly **(c)** cartel **(d)** monopolistically competitive industry. . . . .   ( )a ( )b ( )c ( )d

17. Many oligopolists face a kinked demand curve because **(a)** other producers will follow a price increase but not a decrease **(b)** other producers will generally follow a price decrease but not necessarily a price increase **(c)** other producers will frequently follow neither a price increase nor a decrease **(d)** there is only one firm in the market. . . . .   ( )a ( )b ( )c ( )d

18. Oligopoly is a market structure in which, in the long run,
(a) there may be high profits **(b)** price equals the per-unit cost
of production **(c)** economic efficiency is approached **(d)** all
of these. . . . .   ( )a ( )b ( )c ( )d

Improving the Market Economy

Part 1 — Building Your Economic Vocabulary

Directions: Complete the following crossword puzzle with vocabulary terms from this chapter.

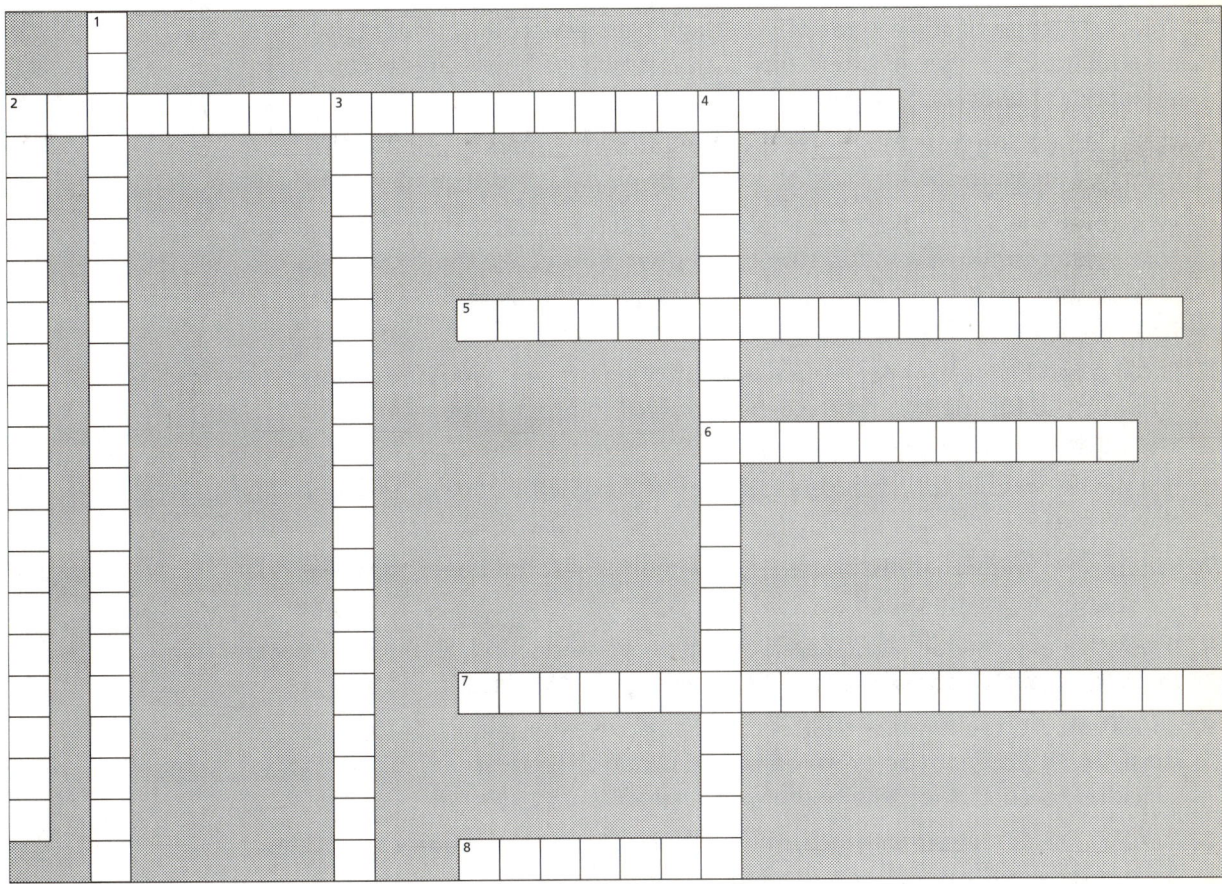

ACROSS

2. the added benefit that individuals directly involved in an activity get from increasing the activity by one unit

5. the principle that one person can keep others from benefiting from a good

6. another word for *spillover*

7. the added cost individuals directly involved in an activity pay to increase the activity by one unit

8. a payment made by government to encourage some activity

DOWN

1. the added benefit that society gets from increasing an activity by one unit

2. the added cost that society pays to increase an activity by one unit

3. the result when *benefits* are shifted to people who are not directly involved with the production or consumption of a good

4. the result when *costs* are shifted to people who are not directly involved with the production or consumption of a good.

Part 2 — Checking Your Economic Knowledge

Directions: Carefully read the following statements. Decide whether the statement is *True* or *False*. Fill in the answer bubble for **T** for *True* or **F** for *False*. If any part of the statement is *False*, then the statement is *False*.

1. Although the market system usually allocates goods and services efficiently among both producers and consumers, it can sometimes cause problems for both groups. . . . .   ( )T ( )F

2. The production of some kinds of goods and services produces negative externalities. A negative externality is an example of how markets can fail in the efficient allocation of goods and services. . . . .   ( )T ( )F

3. When producing goods also produces pollution, the market price of the good does not measure the true cost to society of producing the good. . . . .   ( )T ( )F

4. Whenever the social costs of producing a good are greater than the individual costs, we tend to overproduce the good. If we internalize the social costs of production, the price of the good will rise and consumers will probably demand less of that good. . . . .   ( )T ( )F

5. Forcing producers to install pollution control equipment would probably create an incentive for them to produce more output in order to pay for the new equipment. . . . .   ( )T ( )F

6. It is never possible for producers to benefit from the positive externalities that they produce. . . . .   ( )T ( )F

7. Whenever positive externalities exist, the marginal social benefits are less than the marginal private benefits. . . . .   ( )T ( )F

8. If positive externalities are created by a type of production, the market system tends to allocate too many resources to this type of production. . . . .   ( )T ( )F

9. Education is a process that creates many positive externalities. Since some of these benefits cannot be captured by the producers, government provides subsidies to encourage this kind of production. . . . .   ( )T ( )F

10. Natural monopolies usually occur in industries in which average cost falls as output increases through the range of potential sales. . . . .   ( )T ( )F

Part 3 — Mastering Economic Concepts

Directions: Carefully read the following items. Fill in the answer bubble next to the letter of the *best* answer.

1. The demand curve for a product shows the amount of additional benefit consumers get from each additional unit of the good that they buy. Economists call this **(a)** marginal social utility **(b)** marginal private cost **(c)** marginal private benefit **(d)** incremental pleasure. . . . .   ( )a ( )b ( )c ( )d

2. The supply curve of a firm shows the amount of additional cost to the firm if it produces one more unit of output. Economists call this **(a)** marginal social cost **(b)** marginal social utility **(c)** total social benefit **(d)** marginal private cost . . . .   ( )a ( )b ( )c ( )d

3. From an economic point of view, it is only desirable to produce one additional unit of any specific good or service if **(a)** marginal private costs are greater than marginal private benefits **(b)** marginal private benefits are greater than marginal private costs **(c)** marginal private benefits equal marginal private costs **(d)** both (a) and (c) . . . . ( )a ( )b ( )c ( )d

4. From the point of view of the whole society, goods should be produced up to the point at which **(a)** marginal private cost equals marginal private benefit **(b)** marginal private cost equals total social utility **(c)** total social cost equals total social benefit **(d)** marginal social cost equals marginal private cost. . . . . ( )a ( )b ( )c ( )d

5. Sometimes part of the costs or benefits in a market exchange spill over to third parties not directly involved in the exchange. Economists call these spillovers **(a)** negative externalities **(b)** cost of doing business **(c)** social costs **(d)** externalities . . . . ( )a ( )b ( )c ( )d

6. Whenever costs from spillovers are passed onto third parties in the production of goods or services, **(a)** the marginal social costs to society of providing the good or service are higher than the marginal private costs **(b)** the private costs are greater than the costs to the society of providing the good or service **(c)** both (a) and (b) **(d)** none of these . . . . ( )a ( )b ( )c ( )d

7. Whenever resources are correctly allocated and there are no costs or benefits passed onto third parties outside of the market system, **(a)** marginal social benefit equals marginal private benefit **(b)** marginal social cost equals marginal private cost **(c)** both (a) and (b) **(d)** total social cost equals marginal social utility . . . . ( )a ( )b ( )c ( )d

8. When negative externalities are present, **(a)** MSC = MPC **(b)** MSC > MPC **(c)** MSC < MPC **(d)** MSB = MPB. . . . . ( )a ( )b ( )c ( )d

9. If government passes laws prohibiting pollution, producers will pay higher costs to produce products, which will lead to higher prices, and **(a)** the marginal private cost will rise to be equal with the marginal social cost **(b)** consumers who buy the good will pay the full cost of producing the good **(c)** no external costs will be passed on to third parties not involved in the production or consumption of the good **(d)** all of these . . . . ( )a ( )b ( )c ( )d

10. Assume that there are two different products being made by a single producer in the economy. Producing Product A pollutes the air, but producing Product B does not create any costs that are passed on outside of the market system. Economic theory would say that **(a)** there is an incentive to produce more of Product A than is in the best interest of the entire society **(b)** there is an incentive to produce more of Product B than is in the best interest of the entire society **(c)** both (a) and (b) **(d)** none of these. . . . . ( )a ( )b ( )c ( )d

11. If government taxes each unit of output produced by a polluting firm, the best interest of society would be served by setting that tax equal to **(a)** the difference between marginal social cost and marginal private cost **(b)** $175 **(c)** the difference between marginal social benefit and marginal private cost **(d)** none of these. . . . .   ( )a ( )b ( )c ( )d

12. In the case of positive externalities, **(a)** the marginal social benefits of an activity are less than are the marginal private benefits **(b)** the marginal private benefits of an activity are less than are the marginal social benefits **(c)** the marginal social costs of an activity are greater than are the marginal social benefits **(d)** all of these . . . .   ( )a ( )b ( )c ( )d

13. Of the following, an example of a positive externality is **(a)** the noisy teenagers next door to you going away to college **(b)** your neighbors landscaping their yards **(c)** some residents of your apartment building placing attractive new carpet in the hallways **(d)** all of these . . . .   ( )a ( )b ( )c ( )d

14. An example of a public good that has some positive externalities is **(a)** education **(b)** free public vaccination against chicken pox **(c)** both (a) and (b) **(d)** none of these. . . . .   ( )a ( )b ( )c ( )d

15. From an economic viewpoint, it would be wise to provide those public goods for which **(a)** marginal social benefits are greater than marginal social costs **(b)** marginal social benefits are less than marginal social costs **(c)** private benefits are greater than costs **(d)** there are only negative externalities . . . .   ( )a ( )b ( )c ( )d

16. One way government might effectively encourage the production of goods with positive externalities is to **(a)** tax those goods heavily **(b)** pass laws forbidding companies to produce any goods other than those with positive external benefits **(c)** provide subsidies to the producers of goods with positive externalities **(d)** none of these . . . .   ( )a ( )b ( )c ( )d

17. If government provides low-cost student loans for college students to finance their education, it is **(a)** encouraging the production of education by increasing the demand for education **(b)** discouraging the production of education since taxpayers must bear the cost of the low-cost student loans **(c)** both (a) and (b) **(d)** none of these. . . . .   ( )a ( )b ( )c ( )d

18. Examples of natural monopolies include all of the following *except* **(a)** electric power companies **(b)** water authorities **(c)** oil companies **(d)** natural gas companies . . . .   ( )a ( )b ( )c ( )d

The Labor Market and Determining Personal Income

Part 1 — Building Your Economic Vocabulary

Directions: Match the following terms with the definitions below.

A. closed shop
B. collective bargaining
C. corporate bond rate
D. demand for labor
E. derived demand
F. discount rate
G. equilibrium wage
H. federal funds rate
I. inflation

J. injunction
K. interest
L. labor union
M. minimum wage law
N. monopsony
O. prime rate
P. supply of labor
Q. union shop
R. wage rate

_____ 1. the amount of labor that firms would want to hire at each wage rate

_____ 2. the price paid for each unit of labor

_____ 3. a demand for an input that is dependent on the demand for the product that the input helps to produce

_____ 4. the amount of labor that would be available at each wage rate

_____ 5. the wage rate at which the quantity demanded for labor equals the quantity supplied of labor

_____ 6. a market in which there is only one buyer

_____ 7. a law that sets the lowest wage that can be paid for certain kinds of work

_____ 8. an organization of workers formed to give workers greater bargaining power in their dealings with management

_____ 9. a court order to stop doing something (or to do something)

_____ 10. a business that agrees to hire only those workers who are members of a union

_____ 11. a business that requires workers to join a union shortly after taking a job

_____ 12. the process of having the union negotiate with management to determine the terms of employment for all workers rather than having each worker negotiate separately

_____ 13. the price paid for the use of money

_____ 14. a rise in the average level of prices

_____ 15. the interest rate that banks charge their best corporate customers

_____ 16. the interest rate paid on corporate bonds

_____ 17. the interest rate banks pay to borrow from each other on a short-term basis

_____ 18. the interest rate that banks must pay to borrow from the Federal Reserve System

Part 2 — Checking Your Economic Knowledge

Directions: Carefully read the following statements. Decide whether the statement is *True* or *False*. Fill in the answer bubble for **T** for *True* or **F** for *False*. If any part of the statement is *False*, then the statement is *False*.

1. Economists believe that the demand for labor depends on the demand for the good or service provided. . . . . ( )T ( )F

2. The amount of labor producers will use is inversely related to the wage rate they must pay for labor. . . . . ( )T ( )F

3. In general, there is an inverse relationship between the wage rate and the quantity of labor persons are willing to supply. . . . . ( )T ( )F

4. One of the primary reasons the supply of labor has increased so much in the United States in the last ten years is the increased number of women in the workforce. . . . . ( )T ( )F

5. Unions are generally in favor of increasing the minimum wage because it helps provide low-income families with more money to spend. . . . . ( )T ( )F

6. An increase in the minimum wage increases the amount of labor demanded by companies. . . . . ( )T ( )F

7. If the U.S. Congress passes a new minimum wage law allowing a lower minimum wage for teenagers, this would probably increase the number of teenagers who would get jobs. . . . . ( )T ( )F

8. A yellow-dog contract was a contract workers had to sign before they were hired saying that they would not join a union. . . . . ( )T ( )F

9. Interest can be viewed either as the price we pay to borrow money or the rate of return that a productive piece of machinery earns. . . . . ( )T ( )F

10. In general, the shorter the time period for which a loan is made, the higher the interest rate that will be charged. . . . . ( )T ( )F

11. There is a direct or positive relationship between the risk of making a loan and the interest rate that a lender will receive. . . . . ( )T ( )F

12. The rates charged for consumer credit are usually higher than other rates because consumer loans are often run over a relatively long period of time. . . . . ( )T ( )F

Part 3 — Mastering Economic Concepts

Directions: Carefully read the following items. Fill in the answer bubble next to the letter of the *best* answer.

1. To say that the demand for labor is a derived demand means that the demand for labor depends on **(a)** how much labor is available for sale **(b)** the demand for the final product that is produced using labor as an input **(c)** the price that labor demands **(d)** the number of persons actively looking for jobs . . . . ( )a ( )b ( )c ( )d

2. Because the demand for labor depends heavily on the productivity of labor, **(a)** as the productivity of labor increases, other things held constant, the demand for labor will also rise **(b)** as the productivity of labor falls, other things held constant, the demand for labor rises **(c)** skilled workers generally will be more in demand than unskilled workers **(d)** both (a) and (c) . . . . . ( )a ( )b ( )c ( )d

3. Because the demand curve for labor slopes downward and to the right, **(a)** as the wage rate increases, the quantity demanded of labor increases **(b)** as the wage rate increases, the quantity demanded of labor decreases **(c)** the demand for labor increases at a lower wage rate **(d)** none of these . . . . ( )a ( )b ( )c ( )d

4. The factor that may cause the demand for labor to change is **(a)** a change in the demand for the output **(b)** a change in the productivity of labor **(c)** both (a) and (b) **(d)** none of these . . . . . . ( )a ( )b ( )c ( )d

5. Because the supply of labor curve slopes upward and to the right, **(a)** as wages increase, workers are willing to supply more hours of labor to the market **(b)** there is a positive relationship between the quantity supplied of labor and the wage rate **(c)** if wages decline, workers will supply fewer hours of labor to the market **(d)** all of these . . . . ( )a ( )b ( )c ( )d

6. If the legal minimum wage is set above the market equilibrium wage, **(a)** the quantity demanded of labor will be larger than the quantity supplied **(b)** the quantity supplied of labor will be greater than the quantity demanded **(c)** fewer workers will be willing to supply labor to the market than business would like to hire **(d)** none of these . . . . ( )a ( )b ( )c ( )d

7. The demand for labor will not increase if there is **(a)** an increase in the demand for outputs utilizing labor in their production **(b)** an increase in the productivity of labor **(c)** both (a) and (b) **(d)** an increase in the per hour wage rate of labor . . . . ( )a ( )b ( )c ( )d

8. Equilibrium in the labor market means that **(a)** the amount of labor demanded equals the amount supplied **(b)** the minimum legal wage equals the equilibrium wage **(c)** workers are willing to provide more hours of labor than producers are willing to buy at the market price **(d)** none of these . . . . ( )a ( )b ( )c ( )d

9. The supply of labor would be expected to increase if any of the following occurred *except* **(a)** better or safer working conditions became available to the whole workforce **(b)** many more persons entered the workforce **(c)** the legal working age were lowered to 14 **(d)** the legal minimum wage were increased . . . . ( )a ( )b ( )c ( )d

10. A minimum wage law allowing a lower minimum wage for teenagers than for adults would be likely to mean that **(a)** more teenage workers would be hired **(b)** some adults would lose their jobs **(c)** adult wage rates for unskilled jobs would fall **(d)** all of these. . . . . ( )a ( )b ( )c ( )d

11. If the legal minimum wage were raised from $5 to $15 an hour, **(a)** the quantity demanded of labor would fall **(b)** the quantity supplied of labor would rise **(c)** there would be many more unemployed teenagers **(d)** all of these . . . . ( )a ( )b ( )c ( )d

12. The first labor union in the United States was the **(a)** Noble and Holy Order of the Knights of Labor **(b)** American Federation of Labor **(c)** Congress of Industrial Organizations **(d)** United Auto Workers . . . . ( )a ( )b ( )c ( )d

13. The American Federation of Labor was founded in 1886 by **(a)** George Meany **(b)** Lane Kirkland **(c)** Samuel Gompers **(d)** John L. Lewis. . . . . ( )a ( )b ( )c ( )d

14. The first law stating that union activity did not violate antitrust laws was the **(a)** Norris LaGuardia Act **(b)** Sherman Antitrust Act **(c)** National Labor Relations Act **(d)** Stamp Act . . . . ( )a ( )b ( )c ( )d

15. The act that defined unfair labor practices on the part of unions and outlawed the closed shop was the **(a)** Norris LaGuardia Act **(b)** National Labor Relations Act **(c)** Taft-Hartley Act **(d)** Sherman Antitrust Act. . . . . ( )a ( )b ( )c ( )d

16. In economic terms, interest is **(a)** the price paid for the use of money or credit **(b)** a rate of return earned by a productive piece of machinery **(c)** both (a) and (b) **(d)** none of these. . . . . ( )a ( )b ( )c ( )d

17. It is reasonable to expect producers to invest in productive machinery when **(a)** the rate of return on the machinery exceeds the interest rate at which the firm can borrow money **(b)** the market rate of interest rises above the rate of return on the machinery **(c)** the rate of return on machinery falls below the prime lending rate **(d)** all of these . . . . ( )a ( )b ( )c ( )d

18. Factors that influence the interest rate on loans include all of the following *except* **(a)** the length of time for the loan to be repaid **(b)** the risk of making the loan **(c)** the rate of inflation and cost of making the loan **(d)** the length of time the bank has been in business . . . . ( )a ( )b ( )c ( )d

19. Banks offer loans to their best corporate customers at the **(a)** corporate bond rate **(b)** discount rate **(c)** federal funds rate **(d)** prime rate . . . . ( )a ( )b ( )c ( )d

20. Banks can borrow from the Federal Reserve Bank at the **(a)** federal funds rate **(b)** discount rate **(c)** corporate bond rate **(d)** prime rate . . . . ( )a ( )b ( )c ( )d

Measuring Aggregate Economic Activity

Part 1 — Building Your Economic Vocabulary

Directions: Match the following terms with the definitions below.

A. aggregate demand	**H.** gross domestic product (GDP)
B. aggregate supply	**I.** inflation
C. barter	**J.** investment
D. capital	**K.** macroeconomics
E. constant dollar GDP	**L.** macroeconomic equilibrium
F. consumer goods	**M.** production possibilities curve
G. disposable income	

_____ **1.** the total dollar value of all final goods and services produced by resources located in the United States (regardless of who owns them) during one year's time

_____ **2.** that part of economics that examines the behavior of the whole economy at once

_____ **3.** the economic condition in which the average level of prices goes up

_____ **4.** the value of gross domestic product after taking out the effect of price changes

_____ **5.** a direct trade of goods or services

_____ **6.** a graphic illustration of the combinations of output an economy can produce if all of its resources are utilized and utilized efficiently, given the state of technology

_____ **7.** those items that are made for final consumption

_____ **8.** an increase in the amount of productive capital in an economy

_____ **9.** goods that are produced and can be used as inputs for further production

_____ **10.** the income that is left after deducting tax payments

_____ **11.** the results when the sum of savings and taxes equals the sum of investment and government spending

_____ **12.** the total demand of all people for all goods and services produced in an economy

_____ **13.** the total supply of all goods and services in an economy

Part 2 — Checking Your Economic Knowledge

Directions: Carefully read the following statements. Decide whether the statement is *True* or *False*. Fill in the answer bubble for **T** for *True* or **F** for *False*. If any part of the statement is *False,* then the statement is *False.*

1. In the circular flow diagram of the economy, money flows from households to businesses when households buy goods and services. Money also flows from businesses to households when businesses buy labor and other productive inputs. . . . .   ( )T ( )F

2. Gross domestic product is the amount of all goods and services produced in the economy over the past ten years. . . . .   ( )T ( )F

3. In calculating GDP, final goods are excluded since they are made up of intermediate goods. . . . .   ( )T ( )F

4. GDP is an effective measure of the well-being in an economy because it measures how much of the total goods and services produced are available for each member of the population. . . . .   ( )T ( )F

5. One weakness of GDP as a measure of well-being is that prices can rise over time. This can increase GDP without any real increase in the amount of goods and services produced. . . . .   ( )T ( )F

6. If you took a whole summer to repaint your house yourself, the value of that job would not be included in GDP. . . . .   ( )T ( )F

7. When two individuals barter rather than exchange goods and services for money, the value of this transaction is then included in the calculation of GDP. .   ( )T ( )F

8. GDP cannot measure the quality of goods and services produced. . . . .   ( )T ( )F

9. The total production in the economy is made up of consumer goods, investment goods, and the government sector. . . . .   ( )T ( )F

10. Individuals spend their income primarily on personal consumption, expenditures, investment spending, and the spending of governmental units. . .   ( )T ( )F

11. Individual income is spent primarily on consumption, taxes, and spending. . . . . .   ( )T ( )F

12. Most income is used for consumption. . . . .   ( )T ( )F

13. In order for macroeconomic equilibrium to exist, savings must equal investment plus government spending.. . . . .   ( )T ( )F

Part 3 — Mastering Economic Concepts

Directions: Carefully read the following items. Fill in the answer bubble next to the letter of the *best* answer.

1. Macroeconomics and microeconomics are different in that
   (a) macroeconomics examines the economy as a whole while microeconomics examines specific units in the economy
   (b) macroeconomics examines specific units in the economy while microeconomics examines the economy as a whole
   (c) macroeconomics measures things such as the price of a good and its quantity demanded while microeconomics considers things such as GDP or unemployment **(d)** microeconomics studies inflation and wholesale price levels while macroeconomics studies taxes . . . .   ( )a ( )b ( )c ( )d

2. The macroeconomic model that shows how goods and services as well as resources and money circulate between businesses, households, and governments is the **(a)** circular flow of resources **(b)** linear flow of income **(c)** circular flow diagram of the economy **(d)** circular flow of goods and government . . . .   ( )a ( )b ( )c ( )d

3. GDP does not include the dollar value of intermediate goods that are used as inputs in the production process because **(a)** their value would understate the dollar value of GDP **(b)** their value would then be counted again when the final good was counted and GDP would be overstated **(c)** their value would add nothing to the value of the goods actually produced **(d)** intermediate goods are not really goods that are produced . . . .   ( )a ( )b ( )c ( )d

4. The size of the GDP of a country depends greatly on all of the following *except* **(a)** the amount of natural resources **(b)** the number of people **(c)** the level of skill and education of the workforce **(d)** geographic location. . . . .   ( )a ( )b ( )c ( )d

5. GDP is not a perfect measure because it **(a)** does not consider kinds of items produced **(b)** does not measure the amount produced per person **(c)** does not measure how goods are distributed **(d)** all of these . . . .   ( )a ( )b ( )c ( )d

6. GDP in constant dollars is computed by **(a)** multiplying GDP in current dollars by an adjustment for inflation **(b)** multiplying current GDP by a constant dollar price **(c)** dividing GDP in current dollars by an adjustment for inflation **(d)** dividing GDP in constant dollars by an adjustment for inflation. . . . .   ( )a ( )b ( )c ( )d

7. GDP tends to be lower than the actual value of total goods and services produced because it does not include **(a)** household services such as meals or cleaning **(b)** the quality of items **(c)** unrecorded economic activities such as barters **(d)** all of these. . . . .   ( )a ( )b ( )c ( )d

8. A product that gives the population of an economy satisfaction or utility and yet is not measured in GDP is **(a)** leisure **(b)** taxes **(c)** military goods **(d)** public parks . . . .   ( )a ( )b ( )c ( )d

9. If an economy is using all of its resources efficiently, then **(a)** to increase production of one good means the production of another good must decrease **(b)** to increase production of one good means the production of another good also must increase **(c)** it is producing one type of good and nothing else **(d)** none of these. . . . .   ( )a ( )b ( )c ( )d

10. Points outside the production possibilities curve are not attainable because **(a)** the economy does not have enough resources to produce that level of output **(b)** the government of the economy does not want to produce that much output **(c)** there is not enough demand to encourage producing that amount **(d)** all of these. . . . .   ( )a ( )b ( )c ( )d

11. All of the following are consumer goods *except* **(a)** blankets **(b)** automobiles **(c)** houses occupied by families **(d)** compact disc players . . . . ( )a ( )b ( )c ( )d

12. All of the following are nondurable goods *except* **(a)** milk **(b)** *Business Week* **(c)** a dishwasher **(d)** running shoes . . . . ( )a ( )b ( )c ( )d

13. The major difference between physical investment and financial investment is **(a)** physical investment includes allowances for an improved physical condition of the population **(b)** financial investment includes only factories, machinery, and equipment **(c)** physical investment includes additions to our stock of machines, buildings, and so on, while financial investment refers to buying stocks, bonds, and other securities **(d)** all of these . . . . . ( )a ( )b ( )c ( )d

14. Investment as it is calculated in GDP includes **(a)** new plant and equipment **(b)** inventories **(c)** private housing **(d)** all of these. . . . . ( )a ( )b ( )c ( )d

15. GDP is made up of **(a)** personal consumption, investment expenditures, and government purchases **(b)** taxes, military expenditures, and welfare **(c)** goods, services, and taxes **(d)** savings, income, and taxes . . . . ( )a ( )b ( )c ( )d

16. We use our income for **(a)** savings **(b)** consumption expenditures **(c)** tax payments **(d)** all of these. . . . . ( )a ( )b ( )c ( )d

17. Leakages out of the economy are **(a)** consumption and taxes **(b)** savings and government spending **(c)** taxes and savings **(d)** consumption and savings . . . . ( )a ( )b ( )c ( )d

18. Injections into the economy are **(a)** savings and taxes **(b)** taxes and consumption **(c)** government spending and taxes **(d)** investment and government spending. . . . . ( )a ( )b ( )c ( )d

19. For an economy to be in macroeconomic equilibrium, **(a)** leakages must equal injections **(b)** savings and taxes must equal government spending **(c)** consumption must equal savings and investment **(d)** savings must equal income . . . . ( )a ( )b ( )c ( )d

20. When the economy is in macroeconomic equilibrium, **(a)** aggregate demand equals aggregate savings **(b)** aggregate supply equals aggregate demand **(c)** consumption is higher than savings **(d)** all of these . . . . ( )a ( )b ( )c ( )d

The Distribution of Income

Part 1 — Building Your Economic Vocabulary

Directions: Complete the following crossword puzzle with vocabulary terms from this chapter.

ACROSS

3. _____ distribution of income is how income is shared among people in our society.

5. the average income per person

6. the refusal to hire certain people because of their gender, race, or other characteristics that have nothing to do with their ability to do a job

DOWN

1. _____ distribution of income is the way in which income is divided by economic functions.

2. The _____ _____ of income distribution is a graphic method showing the amount of income inequality that exists in society at any point in time.

4. the condition in which people do not have enough income to provide for their basic needs, such as food, clothing, and shelter

Part 2 — Checking Your Economic Knowledge

Directions: Carefully read the following statements. Decide whether the statement is *True* or *False*. Fill in the answer bubble for **T** for *True* or **F** for *False*. If any part of the statement is *False,* then the statement is *False.*

1. Since the mid-1990s, national income from manufacturing industries has dramatically increased. . . . . ( )T ( )F

2. Labor receives the smallest portion of national income of all the factors of production. . . . . ( )T ( )F

3. The United States has a large and wealthy middle class. . . . . ( )T ( )F

4. You can identify the changes in income inequality by comparing Lorenz curves for different time periods. . . . . ( )T ( )F

5. If the national income in a certain economy is a Lorenz curve that is very close to the line of equality, then income is distributed fairly evenly in that economy. . . . . ( )T ( )F

6. Poverty comes about in the United States economy because we do not produce enough goods and services for everyone to have some minimum decent standard of living. . . . . ( )T ( )F

7. Poverty is about equally distributed over our population among the different races. . . . . ( )T ( )F

8. In the United States, the percentage of urban and suburban families living in poverty is higher than the percentage of rural families. . . . . ( )T ( )F

9. The education of the head of the family has very little to do with the chances of the family's being below the poverty level. . . . . ( )T ( )F

10. One of the primary causes of poverty is high unemployment. . . . . ( )T ( )F

Part 3 — Mastering Economic Concepts

Directions: Carefully read the following items. Fill in the answer bubble next to the letter of the *best* answer.

1. When economists say that we are a rich nation, they are referring to the fact that **(a)** 80 percent of American families own at least one car **(b)** the vast majority of homes have a TV set and refrigerator **(c)** luxuries such as air-conditioners or washing machines are owned by the vast majority of the population **(d)** all of these . . . . ( )a ( )b ( )c ( )d

2. In terms of the share of national income that they produce, two of the fastest growing sectors in the U.S. economy are **(a)** manufacturing and mining **(b)** mining and construction **(c)** transportation and manufacturing **(d)** government and services . . . . ( )a ( )b ( )c ( )d

3. Functional distribution of income measures income as it is distributed among **(a)** land, labor, capital, and entrepreneurship **(b)** families in the economy **(c)** businesses in the economy **(d)** none of these . . . . ( )a ( )b ( )c ( )d

4. The largest single part of our national income is paid in the form of **(a)** wages to workers for their labor **(b)** profits to business managers **(c)** interest to borrow financial capital **(d)** rents to landlords or landowners. . . . . ( )a ( )b ( )c ( )d

5. In 1990, the U.S. economy produced enough national income that if it were distributed equally among every man, woman, and child, each would have received approximately **(a)** $1,300 **(b)** $3,000 **(c)** $22,000 **(d)** $39,000. . . . . ( )a ( )b ( )c ( )d

6. Personal distribution of income measures income in the economy as it is distributed **(a)** by economic function such as in wages, interest, rents, or profits **(b)** among families in the economy **(c)** among land, labor, capital, and entrepreneurship **(d)** all of these. . . . . ( )a ( )b ( )c ( )d

7. Income in the United States is distributed in such a way that **(a)** most persons receive about an equal share **(b)** almost all the income is held by less than 2 percent of the population **(c)** a large middle class (approximately 57 percent) enjoys family incomes between $35,000 and $75,000 **(d)** poverty really does not exist in the economy . . . . ( )a ( )b ( )c ( )d

8. The Lorenz curve is a graphic relationship between **(a)** the cumulative percentage of households in the United States and the cumulative percentage of income that they receive **(b)** the percentage of families in the United States and the percentage of income that they receive **(c)** the percentage of individuals in the United States and the percentage of wealth (assets) they hold **(d)** wealth and poverty . . . . ( )a ( )b ( )c ( )d

9. When a Lorenz curve is highly bowed outward away from the 45 degree line, it is an indication of a highly **(a)** equal distribution of income **(b)** unequal distribution of income **(c)** equal distribution of wealth (assets) **(d)** unequal distribution of wealth (assets) . . . . . ( )a ( )b ( )c ( )d

10. In the United States, poverty could be permanently eliminated by **(a)** government programs such as President Johnson's Great Society Program **(b)** simply giving every American an equal share of the nation's income **(c)** the War on Poverty program **(d)** none of these. . . . . ( )a ( )b ( )c ( )d

11. The official poverty level of income in the United States is determined by the U.S. Department of Agriculture based primarily upon **(a)** the cost of housing, medical services, and education **(b)** rents, taxes, and the cost of government **(c)** the cost of a nutritious low-cost diet **(d)** the occupation of the chief breadwinner in the family . . . . ( )a ( )b ( )c ( )d

12. Characteristics of those persons in our economy who would qualify as poor include **(a)** equal distribution of whites and nonwhites **(b)** equal distribution of families headed by both males and females **(c)** equal distribution of those both with and without a great deal of formal education **(d)** unusually large representation of nonwhites, female heads of households, and holders of little formal education . . . .   ( )a ( )b ( )c ( )d

13. Most causes of poverty can be classified into which of the following categories? **(a)** unemployment **(b)** low productivity **(c)** restrictions on job entry **(d)** all of these . . . .   ( )a ( )b ( )c ( )d

14. A major cause of poverty in the United States economy is **(a)** large numbers of persons who would rather be poor than work for a living **(b)** employers who do not want to give jobs to poor persons **(c)** unemployment due to low levels of economic activity in the economy **(d)** not enough national income to provide a decent standard of living for the whole population . . . .   ( )a ( )b ( )c ( )d

15. The unemployment problem in our economy is aggravated by all of the following factors *except* **(a)** restrictive apprenticeship programs by unions **(b)** discrimination against people by race, gender, or other factors **(c)** a lack of training opportunities for candidates who would like to seek skilled jobs **(d)** the Manpower Development Training Act . . . .   ( )a ( )b ( )c ( )d

16. Over the last 50 years, government programs to aid the poor have had the goal of **(a)** creating jobs for the poor **(b)** educating and retraining the poor **(c)** income support for the poor **(d)** all of these . . . .   ( )a ( )b ( )c ( )d

Unemployment

Part 1 — Building Your Economic Vocabulary

Directions: Complete the following crossword puzzle with vocabulary terms from this chapter.

ACROSS

3. _____ unemployment is that part of unemployment made up of people who are out of work because of factors that vary with the time of year.

6. the total number of people in the working age group (16 years and over) who are either employed or actively seeking work

8. _____ unemployment is unemployment resulting from too low a level of aggregate demand.

9. the percentage of the civilian labor force that is considered unemployed

10. the condition of those who are willing and able to work and are actively seeking work but who do not currently work

DOWN

1. _____ unemployment is unemployment of people who are temporarily between jobs.

2. _____ employment is the employment of about 95 percent of the labor force.

4. _____ unemployment is unemployment resulting from skills that do not match what employers require or from being geographically separated from job opportunities.

5. the condition in which unemployment is high and GDP falls for two or more quarters

7. The _____ Act of 1946 states that the federal government should take responsibility for full employment, price stability, and economic growth.

Part 2 — Checking Your Economic Knowledge

Directions: Carefully read the following statements. Decide whether the statement is *True* or *False*. Fill in the answer bubble for **T** for *True* or **F** for *False*. If any part of the statement is *False*, then the statement is *False*.

1. If you are independently wealthy and choose not to work, you will be counted among the unemployed of our economy.. . . . . ( )T ( )F

2. Unemployment is usually measured as the percentage of the civilian labor force that is currently unemployed. . . . . ( )T ( )F

3. The unemployment rate is about the same throughout the United States and about the same for people of all races, genders, and age groups. . . . . ( )T ( )F

4. The group within our economy that experiences the highest unemployment rate is the age group from 16 through 19. . . . . ( )T ( )F

5. A recession is defined as the condition in which unemployment is high and GDP falls for two or more consecutive quarters. . . . . ( )T ( )F

6. Persons without any education or training who are looking for jobs could be considered structurally unemployed. . . . . ( )T ( )F

7. When aggregate demand decreases, cyclical unemployment increases. . . . . ( )T ( )F

8. John Barber earns his living each year as a professional golfer in Michigan. During the winter months, he could be considered seasonally unemployed. . . . . ( )T ( )F

9. Full employment is considered to be about 95 percent employment because 5 percent is allowed for structural unemployment. . . . . ( )T ( )F

10. If the help-wanted ads are full of openings for plumbers but not for welders, then welders looking for a job at that time would be frictionally unemployed.. . ( )T ( )F

Part 3 — Mastering Economic Concepts

Directions: Carefully read the following items. Fill in the answer bubble next to the letter of the *best* answer.

1. The civilian labor force excludes all of the following *except* **(a)** members of the armed services **(b)** prisoners **(c)** government workers **(d)** people in mental hospitals . . . . ( )a ( )b ( )c ( )d

2. The civilian labor force includes **(a)** all employed persons as well as all those over 16 who are actively seeking employment **(b)** all nonmilitary employed persons and all those over 16 who are looking for work but are not yet employed **(c)** all nonmilitary persons who are looking for work **(d)** all those over 16 who are looking for work . . . . ( )a ( )b ( )c ( )d

3. Economists define the unemployment rate as **(a)** the percentage of the population that is unemployed **(b)** the percentage of the total labor force that is unemployed **(c)** the percentage of the total civilian labor force that is unemployed **(d)** the rate at which the number of unemployed persons is rising. . . . . ( )a ( )b ( )c ( )d

4. The official unemployment rate is figured by dividing **(a)** the number of people employed by the number in the civilian labor force **(b)** the number of people in the civilian labor force by the number of unemployed **(c)** the number employed by the number unemployed **(d)** none of these. . . . . ( )a ( )b ( )c ( )d

5. The Bureau of Labor Statistics reports the official unemployment rate, but this rate does not include **(a)** those who have given up looking for jobs but still would like to have jobs **(b)** those who have part-time jobs but would like to have full-time jobs **(c)** hidden unemployment **(d)** all of these . . . . ( )a ( )b ( )c ( )d

6. Of the following statements, the one that is most true about the distribution of unemployment in our economy is that it is **(a)** higher among nonwhites, women, and the young **(b)** highest among young, white, male workers **(c)** lowest among nonwhite females **(d)** about equally distributed among people of all age groups, genders, and races. . . . . ( )a ( )b ( )c ( )d

7. Unemployment hurts the economy because **(a)** it makes people unhappy **(b)** it causes taxes to rise **(c)** unemployed persons are not adding to GDP **(d)** none of these. . . . . ( )a ( )b ( )c ( )d

8. The Employment Act of 1946 was a commitment by the Congress of the United States to **(a)** provide jobs for everyone willing and able to work **(b)** pursue economic policies that would promote maximum levels of employment in the economy **(c)** make payments to unemployed persons to ease the burden of unemployment **(d)** force businesses to hire all those workers who were willing, able, and suitably skilled to work . . . . ( )a ( )b ( )c ( )d

9. A recession occurs when **(a)** unemployment is very high and prices rise faster than the unemployment rate **(b)** GDP declines for two consecutive quarters and unemployment rises **(c)** inflation is very high and unemployment rises **(d)** none of these . . . . ( )a ( )b ( )c ( )d

10. When the jobs that are available require either basic or even specialized skills that the people looking for work do not have, there is **(a)** cyclical unemployment **(b)** structural unemployment **(c)** frictional unemployment **(d)** none of these . . . . ( )a ( )b ( )c ( )d

11. When there is not enough demand for goods and services in the economy, producers reduce their level of production, causing **(a)** seasonal unemployment **(b)** cyclical unemployment **(c)** structural unemployment **(d)** none of these . . . . ( )a ( )b ( )c ( )d

12. Frictional unemployment occurs when workers **(a)** do not have employable skills **(b)** have employable skills but are either between jobs or have not yet started their first jobs after completing school or training **(c)** are unemployed because their work is not in demand during certain seasons **(d)** do not really want jobs . . . . ( )a ( )b ( )c ( )d

13. Some kinds of industries use many workers at certain times and very few workers at other times of the year. This type of unemployment is **(a)** structural **(b)** cyclical **(c)** seasonal **(d)** none of these. . . . .   ( )a ( )b ( )c ( )d

14. Frictional and seasonal unemployment **(a)** are of less social concern because they last a short time **(b)** make up about 5 percent of unemployment when there is full employment **(c)** both (a) and (b) **(d)** none of these. . . . .   ( )a ( )b ( )c ( )d

15. Economists consider the civilian labor force to be fully employed when **(a)** all members have jobs **(b)** about 85 percent is employed **(c)** about 95 percent is employed **(d)** none of these . . . .   ( )a ( )b ( )c ( )d

16. Structural unemployment can be reduced in all of the following ways *except* by **(a)** reducing educational requirements for jobs that require less education **(b)** developing training programs to raise the skill level of the available workers **(c)** reducing the minimum wage **(d)** reducing government subsidies to businesses for on-the-job training programs. . . . .   ( )a ( )b ( )c ( )d

17. The overall trend in the employment rates in the United States is **(a)** downward **(b)** constant **(c)** upward **(d)** inconsistent . . . .   ( )a ( )b ( )c ( )d

Inflation

Part 1 — Building Your Economic Vocabulary

Directions: Complete each of the following sentences with chapter vocabulary from the list below.

Consumer Price Index (CPI)   demand-pull inflation
cost-push inflation   fixed income
creditors   inflation
debtors   price index
deflation   speculation

1. A _____ is an income that is set and does not change from year to year.

2. People who have borrowed money from someone else are called _____.

3. _____ is a sustained rise in the general level of prices.

4. _____ occurs when someone buys a large amount of a good and hopes to resell it at a much higher price.

5. _____ are people who have loaned money to others.

6. A number that compares prices in one year with some earlier base year is a _____.

7. A number used to calculate changes in the average level of prices for a number of items typically bought by urban families is the _____.

8. _____ is a decline in the average level of prices.

9. A rise in the general level of prices that is caused by increased costs of making and selling goods is _____.

10. A rise in the general level of prices caused by too high a level of aggregate demand in relation to aggregate supply is _____.

Part 2 — Checking Your Economic Knowledge

Directions: Carefully read the following statements. Decide whether the statement is *True* or *False*. Fill in the answer bubble for **T** for *True* or **F** for *False*. If any part of the statement is *False*, then the statement is *False*.

1. Inflation is a rise in the general price level of goods and services and not necessarily a rise in the price of just one commodity.. . . . . ( )T ( )F

2. Inflation is a problem only in the United States. . . . . ( )T ( )F

3. In general, unexpected inflation hurts the debtor and aids the creditor. . . . . ( )T ( )F

4. Inflation hurts those people on fixed incomes more than it does any other group. . . . . ( )T ( )F

5. The Consumer Price Index is one means by which inflation is measured. . . . . ( )T ( )F

6. The Consumer Price Index in 1990 was 130.7, which means that prices in 1990 were more than double prices in the previous year. . . . . ( )T ( )F

7. One problem with using the Consumer Price Index as a measure of inflation is that it does not measure the cost of living for any one specific individual.. . . . . . . ( )T ( )F

8. Two types of inflation are cost-pull and demand-push. . . . . ( )T ( )F

9. During a period of deflation, the prices of all goods fall to a new low price.. . . . ( )T ( )F

Part 3 — Mastering Economic Concepts

Directions: Carefully read the following items. Fill in the answer bubble next to the letter of the *best* answer.

1. Inflation is defined as **(a)** an increase in the price of a good or service that we buy **(b)** a cause of uncertainty in the marketplace **(c)** a sustained rise in the general level of prices **(d)** all of these . . . ( )a ( )b ( )c ( )d

2. Inflation can cause **(a)** uncertainty among both buyers and producers **(b)** higher real profits and increased employment when it is quite mild **(c)** unemployment and reduced demand when it is quite high **(d)** all of these. . . . . ( )a ( )b ( )c ( )d

3. Inflation can lead to **(a)** a sharp decline in the rate of unemployment **(b)** speculation **(c)** greater economic efficiency **(d)** all of these . . . . ( )a ( )b ( )c ( )d

4. The effect of unexpected inflation on loans is that **(a)** debtors can gain from inflation **(b)** creditors can be hurt by inflation **(c)** both (a) and (b) **(d)** workers will benefit from inflation. . . . . ( )a ( )b ( )c ( )d

5. Persons living on fixed incomes, such as retirees, **(a)** benefit from inflation **(b)** are hurt by inflation **(c)** are not affected by inflation **(d)** receive more income during periods of inflation . . . . ( )a ( )b ( )c ( )d

6. Inflation can **(a)** make people work in more productive ways **(b)** cause more efficient allocation of the economy's resources **(c)** make planning difficult for businesses **(d)** none of these . . . . . . ( )a ( )b ( )c ( )d

7. If you had $50,000 in the bank in a savings account and the inflation rate was very high, you would benefit most from **(a)** leaving the $50,000 in the bank **(b)** investing in other assets whose value would increase with the rate of inflation **(c)** taking the money out of the bank and keeping it hidden in your home **(d)** buying high-risk stocks and bonds . . . .   ( )a ( )b ( )c ( )d

8. Of the following items, those not included in the goods used to figure the CPI are **(a)** government services **(b)** taxes **(c)** military weapons **(d)** all of these. . . . .   ( )a ( )b ( )c ( )d

9. The Consumer Price Index is a technical means of measuring **(a)** the rate of inflation over a period of time **(b)** the rate of consumer demand **(c)** the unemployment rate **(d)** the amount of recession in the economy. . . . .   ( )a ( )b ( )c ( )d

10. The Consumer Price Index shows what percentage the price of a number of typical items is of **(a)** the cost of living **(b)** real GDP **(c)** inflation **(d)** the prices of these same typical items in some base year . . . .   ( )a ( )b ( )c ( )d

11. The shortcomings of the Consumer Price Index as a measure of the cost of living include all of the following *except* **(a)** it does not measure the cost of living for any one individual in the economy **(b)** it includes only items bought and sold in the market **(c)** it does not account for changes in the quality of goods, only their prices **(d)** it does not measure how fast prices can rise or fall . . . .   ( )a ( )b ( )c ( )d

12. The goods that the Bureau of Labor Statistics uses to calculate the CPI include **(a)** all consumer goods and services **(b)** a representative market basket of consumer goods weighted by their importance in the average consumer budget **(c)** housing, food, transportation, and clothing only **(d)** food, beverages, and necessities only. . . . .   ( )a ( )b ( )c ( )d

13. When consumers try to buy goods faster than businesses are able to make them, the resulting inflation is **(a)** cost-push **(b)** deflation **(c)** on the supply side **(d)** demand-pull.   ( )a ( )b ( )c ( )d

14. An example of cost-push inflation would be **(a)** an increase in the minimum wage **(b)** insulating your house to lower your heating bills **(c)** too high a demand for microcomputers in relation to the supply **(d)** an increase in the price of cars to compensate for increases in federally required safety features. . . . .   ( )a ( )b ( )c ( )d

15. When there is demand-pull inflation, the aggregate demand curve shifts up and to the right **(a)** the same amount the supply curve shifts **(b)** while the supply curve remains the same **(c)** less than the supply curve shifts **(d)** more than the supply curve shifts .   ( )a ( )b ( )c ( )d

16. The inflation caused by a quick rise in the cost of raw materials and capital equipment is called **(a)** cost-push **(b)** demand-pull **(c)** deflation **(d)** cost-of-living inflation . . . .   ( )a ( )b ( )c ( )d

17. We attempt to control demand-pull inflation mainly by
(a) freeing the supply of resources from artificial controls
(b) enforcing antitrust legislation **(c)** using monetary and
fiscal policy **(d)** all of these. . . . .   ( )a   ( )b   ( )c   ( )d

18. To try to control cost-push inflation, we should **(a)** reduce the
control of special interest groups over important raw materials
(b) strengthen and enforce antitrust legislation **(c)** free resource
prices of artificial limits **(d)** all of these . . . .   ( )a   ( )b   ( )c   ( )d

Money, the Federal Reserve System, and Banking

Part 1 — Building Your Economic Vocabulary

Directions: Match the following terms with the definitions below.

A. asset demand for money
B. Board of Governors
C. check
D. commercial bank
E. credit union
F. currency
G. demand deposit
H. Federal Advisory Council
I. Federal Deposit Insurance Corporation (FDIC)

J. Federal Open Market Committee (FOMC)
K. Federal Reserve System (the Fed)
L. financial intermediary
M. member banks
N. mutual savings banks
O. savings and loan association
P. share draft account
Q. transaction demand for money

_____ **1.** a written order to pay money from amounts deposited

_____ **2.** the demand for money in order to hold wealth in the form of money

_____ **3.** those banks that belong to the Federal Reserve System

_____ **4.** the agency that insures deposits of individuals and businesses for up to $100,000 in the event of bank failure

_____ **5.** a financial intermediary that mainly provides a place for people to save money and lends that money to people to buy houses or other things

_____ **6.** a financial intermediary formed around something that its members have in common

_____ **7.** the demand for money to make exchanges

_____ **8.** the central banking system in the United States

_____ **9.** money that must be paid upon demand by the holder of a check

_____ **10.** an account with a credit union from which withdrawals can be made easily using a draft

_____ **11.** an organization that helps the flow of money from people with money to save to people who need to borrow money

_____ **12.** banks that were first formed for the same reasons as savings and loan associations and that promote thrift by their members

_____ **13.** coins and paper money

_____ **14.** the part of the Federal Reserve System that acts on one of the most important parts of monetary policy—the buying and selling of U.S. government securities by the Federal Reserve Banks

_____ **15.** a group that consists of 12 members who meet four times each year with the Board of Governors to discuss the economic situation and policies of the board

_____ **16.** a type of financial institution that was originally formed to serve businesses, but now provides a large number of financial services to both business customers and individuals

_____ **17.** a group that supervises the Federal Reserve System

Part 2 — Checking Your Economic Knowledge

Directions: Carefully read the following statements. Decide whether the statement is *True* or *False*. Fill in the answer bubble for **T** for *True* or **F** for *False*. If any part of the statement is *False*, then the statement is *False*.

1. Sometimes there is very little difference between money and near monies when economists talk about what is money. . . . . ( )T ( )F

2. The major reason money has developed in modern economies is that it eliminates the need for barter, making exchange much quicker and easier. . . . . . ( )T ( )F

3. When money instead of other goods or services is acceptable to both trading partners in an exchange, money is functioning as a medium of exchange. . . . . . . ( )T ( )F

4. When we measure the value of goods and services in terms of dollars, we are using money as a store of value. . . . . ( )T ( )F

5. If the money supply is held constant and the demand for money increases, it would be reasonable to expect the market interest rate to rise. . . . . ( )T ( )F

6. If we save our money for some future purchase, we are using money as a measure of value. . . . . ( )T ( )F

7. The demand for money has two parts, the transaction demand and the asset demand. . . . . ( )T ( )F

8. Consumers control the money supply in the U.S. economy because they decide what to purchase. . . . . ( )T ( )F

9. The Board of Governors of the Federal Reserve System is made up of 12 members who are the presidents of the 12 district banks. . . . . ( )T ( )F

10. Commercial banks provide financial services exclusively to businesses and business customers. . . . . ( )T ( )F

11. Because of the FDIC, most depositors have suffered no financial lapses when banks have had to close. . . . . ( )T ( )F

12. Nonbank financial intermediaries provide customers with many of the same financial services as banks do. . . . . ( )T ( )F

Part 3 — Mastering Economic Concepts

Directions: Carefully read the following items. Fill in the answer bubble next to the letter of the *best* answer.

1. Checks frequently are used as money in our economy for all of the following types of payments *except* **(a)** mail-order purchases **(b)** mortgage payments **(c)** purchases for which buyers require proof that they paid for the goods or services received **(d)** purchase of food items through vending machines. . . . . ( )a ( )b ( )c ( )d

2. Of the money used in our economy, coins and paper currency make up about **(a)** 90 percent **(b)** 50 percent **(c)** 30 percent **(d)** 10 percent. . . . . ( )a ( )b ( )c ( )d

3. Forms of money, such as savings accounts, that can be changed into currency or checking account deposits very quickly and easily, are called **(a)** charge cards **(b)** near money **(c)** quick money **(d)** transaction money . . . . ( )a ( )b ( )c ( )d

4. All modern industrial economies have developed some form of money because **(a)** money makes the economics of exchange much easier **(b)** barter is more difficult **(c)** money serves as a medium of exchange **(d)** all of these . . . . ( )a ( )b ( )c ( )d

5. For money to serve as a medium of exchange, it must be **(a)** foldable **(b)** acceptable to the parties trying to exchange **(c)** declared by government to be the official money **(d)** acceptable to one party trying to exchange. . . . . ( )a ( )b ( )c ( )d

6. The Susan B. Anthony dollar is a good example of **(a)** money that served as an excellent medium of exchange **(b)** money declared official by government but unacceptable as a medium of exchange to many trading parties **(c)** near money **(d)** plastic money. . . . . ( )a ( )b ( )c ( )d

7. When money functions as a measure of value, it **(a)** allows us to compare different goods and services on the same basis of money price **(b)** allows trading parties to communicate more clearly what they expect in return for their goods or services **(c)** both (a) and (b) **(d)** none of these. . . . . ( )a ( )b ( )c ( )d

8. Money serves as a store of value because **(a)** it enables us to reserve its purchasing power for the future **(b)** it holds its value to some extent over time **(c)** both (a) and (b) **(d)** it circulates through stores and small shops . . . . ( )a ( )b ( )c ( )d

9. As income in the economy rises, we expect **(a)** the transaction demand for money to rise **(b)** the transaction demand for money to fall **(c)** the transaction demand for money to stay about the same **(d)** the asset demand for money to fall . . . . ( )a ( )b ( )c ( )d

10. The demand for money comes from **(a)** the desire of consumers to use money to make exchanges **(b)** the desire of consumers to hold money as an asset **(c)** the desire of workers to earn more money **(d)** both (a) and (b). . . . . ( )a ( )b ( )c ( )d

11. As interest rates in the economy rise, we expect **(a)** the asset demand for money to rise **(b)** the asset demand for money to stay about the same **(c)** the transaction demand for money to fall **(d)** the asset demand for money to fall. . . . . ( )a ( )b ( )c ( )d

12. The supply of money in the U.S. economy is controlled primarily by **(a)** consumers **(b)** the U.S. Treasury **(c)** the Federal Reserve System **(d)** businesses . . . . ( )a ( )b ( )c ( )d

13. The interest rates that exist in the market are determined by **(a)** the forces of supply and demand in the money markets **(b)** the Treasurer of the U.S. **(c)** commercial banks **(d)** savings and loan associations . . . . ( )a ( )b ( )c ( )d

14. The Federal Reserve System was established **(a)** just before the Bank of England **(b)** in 1913 through the Federal Reserve Act **(c)** as 12 separate banks that would each act as the central bank for a given part of the country **(d)** both (b) and (c). . . . . ( )a ( )b ( )c ( )d

15. The Federal Reserve System includes all of the following *except* **(a)** all national banks **(b)** the 12 Federal Reserve District Banks **(c)** all state-chartered banks **(d)** the Board of Governors . . . .   ( )a   ( )b   ( )c   ( )d

16. The members of the Board of Governors of the Federal Reserve System **(a)** are appointed by the president of the United States **(b)** are appointed for 14-year terms **(c)** have a great deal of power to influence monetary policy in our economy **(d)** all of these . . . .   ( )a   ( )b   ( )c   ( )d

17. The Federal Open Market Committee (FOMC) of the Federal Reserve System is responsible for **(a)** controlling the buying and selling of U.S. government securities by the Federal Reserve Banks **(b)** determining how much the government of the United States can borrow from the Federal Reserve System **(c)** controlling how much credit consumers can utilize on their charge cards **(d)** all of these . . . .   ( )a   ( )b   ( )c   ( )d

18. The major functions of the Federal Reserve System include all of the following *except* **(a)** serving as a banker's bank **(b)** issuing currency and clearing checks **(c)** controlling the money supply and acting as a bank for government accounts **(d)** keeping interest rates low by printing money . . . .   ( )a   ( )b   ( )c   ( )d

19. Commercial banks are banks that **(a)** issue credit cards and sell travelers checks **(b)** offer checking and savings accounts and make loans **(c)** rent out safety deposit boxes and exchange foreign currency **(d)** all of these . . . .   ( )a   ( )b   ( )c   ( )d

20. Bank charters are granted to **(a)** national banks by the federal government **(b)** national banks by the Federal Advisory Council **(c)** state banks by a state government **(d)** both (a) and (c) . . . .   ( )a   ( )b   ( )c   ( )d

21. The most important contribution of the Federal Deposit Insurance Corporation (FDIC) to the banking system in the United States has been that it **(a)** arranges mergers between two or more failing banks **(b)** insures deposits of every commercial bank for up to $100,000 per deposit account **(c)** increases stability in the banking system by increasing confidence **(d)** increases the risk of holding money in bank accounts . . . .   ( )a   ( )b   ( )c   ( )d

22. Nonbank financial intermediaries include all of the following *except* **(a)** savings and loan associations **(b)** mutual savings banks **(c)** fire insurance companies **(d)** life insurance companies . . . .   ( )a   ( )b   ( )c   ( )d

Monetary Policy

Part 1 — Building Your Economic Vocabulary

Directions: Complete the following crossword puzzle with vocabulary terms from this chapter.

ACROSS

2. the difference between actual reserves and required reserves

6. A _____ monetary policy is a policy of the Fed that causes the money supply to decrease.

7. A _____ reserve banking system is a system in which banks must keep some fraction or part of their deposits in the form of reserves.

11. _____ time lag: The time it takes to decide on a policy.

12. A federal _____ rate is the interest rate that banks pay for short term loans that they make to one another.

13. the fraction of deposits that the Fed determines banks must keep on reserve

DOWN

1. the number that expresses the relationship between a change in bank reserves and the change in the money supply

3. the dollar amount banks must keep on reserve

4. the changing of the amount of money in the economy in order to reduce unemployment, keep prices stable, and promote economic growth

5. the buying and selling of U.S. government securities by the Federal Reserve

8. A _____ monetary policy is a policy of the Fed that causes the money supply to rise.

9. _____ time lag: The time it takes for the effects of a policy change to be completely felt in the economy.

10. A discount _____ is the interest rate banks must pay when they borrow money from the Fed.

Part 2 — Checking Your Economic Knowledge

Directions: Carefully read the following statements. Decide whether the statement is *True* or *False*. Fill in the answer bubble for **T** for *True* or **F** for *False*. If any part of the statement is *False*, then the statement is *False*.

1. The required reserve ratio is the percentage of total deposits a bank is required to hold in reserve. . . . .   ( )T ( )F

2. When a bank has loaned out all of its required reserves, economists say that the bank is loaned up. . . . .   ( )T ( )F

3. If the demand for money rises and the supply of money increases at the same time, it would be possible to have either increasing or decreasing interest rates, depending on the size of the increases. . . . .   ( )T ( )F

4. A tight monetary policy occurs when the Federal Reserve System increases the money supply to drive up interest rates. . . . .   ( )T ( )F

5. A loose monetary policy occurs when the Federal Reserve System reduces the money supply to drive down interest rates. . . . .   ( )T ( )F

6. The size of the deposit expansion multiplier depends greatly upon the size of the required reserve ratio. . . . .   ( )T ( )F

7. An increase in the discount rate refers to the fact that commercial banks will not offer discounts on the prices they charge for their services. . . . .   ( )T ( )F

8. High interest rates usually increase the desire of businesses to hold large inventories. . . . .   ( )T ( )F

9. A reduction in the interest rate would reduce the desire and ability of many individuals to build houses.. . . . .   ( )T ( )F

10. Inside time lag, the time it takes for the effects of a monetary policy change to be felt in the economy, may take from six months to 24 months. . . . .   ( )T ( )F

Part 3 — Mastering Economic Concepts

Directions: Carefully read the following items. Fill in the answer bubble next to the letter of the *best* answer.

1. The quantity of money that both individuals and businesses demand will **(a)** increase as interest rates increase **(b)** decrease as interest rates increase **(c)** increase as interest rates decrease **(d)** both (b) and (c) . . . . ( )a ( )b ( )c ( )d

2. In general, the demand for money increases when **(a)** the wealth of the economy grows **(b)** the prices we pay for goods fall **(c)** interest rates rise **(d)** banks make fewer loans . . . . ( )a ( )b ( )c ( )d

3. A fractional reserve banking system is one in which **(a)** money is printed in fractional dollar amounts **(b)** all of the deposits remain with the bank in which they were deposited **(c)** only a fraction of the total deposits are kept by the bank in the form of reserves **(d)** banks loan out all of the money that is deposited with them. . ( )a ( )b ( )c ( )d

4. Two important factors that influence the amount of total deposits banks have are **(a)** the interest rate and the reserve requirement of the Fed **(b)** the reserves they have and the reserve requirement of the Fed **(c)** the interest rate they pay on savings accounts and the interest rate they charge on loans **(d)** none of these . . . . ( )a ( )b ( )c ( )d

5. A single bank system with a 20 percent required reserve ratio can create deposits equal to its original deposits times a multiple of **(a)** three **(b)** 20 **(c)** two **(d)** five. . . . . ( )a ( )b ( )c ( )d

6. The excess reserves of a bank are equal to **(a)** required reserves minus actual reserves **(b)** actual reserves minus required reserves **(c)** actual reserves plus required reserves **(d)** none of these . . . . . . ( )a ( )b ( )c ( )d

7. The market rate of interest is determined primarily by **(a)** the supply of and demand for money **(b)** direct orders from the Fed **(c)** the rate banks pay on checking account deposits **(d)** the consumer demand for money . . . . ( )a ( )b ( )c ( )d

8. Whenever the Federal Reserve System is expanding the money supply, it is following **(a)** a tight monetary policy **(b)** a loose monetary policy **(c)** a loose fiscal policy **(d)** a tight fiscal policy. . . . ( )a ( )b ( )c ( )d

9. If the Federal Reserve System reduced the required reserve ratio, it would be **(a)** expanding the money supply **(b)** following a loose monetary policy **(c)** both (a) and (b) **(d)** reducing the money supply . . . . ( )a ( )b ( )c ( )d

10. The deposit expansion multiplier is computed by dividing **(a)** the number one by the reserve ratio **(b)** the reserve ratio by the number one **(c)** excess reserves by required reserves **(d)** required reserves by excess reserves . . . . ( )a ( )b ( )c ( )d

11. If the Federal Reserve System raised the discount rate, this would have the effect of **(a)** reducing the money supply **(b)** producing a tight monetary policy **(c)** both (a) and (b) **(d)** none of these . . . . . .   ( )a ( )b ( )c ( )d

12. In open market operations, the Federal Reserve System expands the money supply by **(a)** selling U.S. government securities on the open market **(b)** buying U.S. corporate bonds from banks and individuals **(c)** buying U.S. government securities from the public **(d)** selling U.S. savings bonds to the public . . . .   ( )a ( )b ( )c ( )d

13. If the money supply is expanded, interest rates **(a)** may fall and businesses may begin to increase their borrowing **(b)** may rise and businesses may begin to increase their borrowing **(c)** may fall and borrowing may fall **(d)** none of these . . . .   ( )a ( )b ( )c ( )d

14. Tight monetary policy generally will **(a)** increase interest rates and reduce borrowing and aggregate demand **(b)** reduce interest rates and borrowing and increase aggregate demand **(c)** increase economic growth and reduce interest rates **(d)** reduce economic growth and increase aggregate demand . . . .   ( )a ( )b ( )c ( )d

15. During periods of high interest rates, business inventories usually are **(a)** larger than during periods of low interest rates **(b)** smaller than during periods of low interest rates **(c)** about the same as during periods of low interest rates **(d)** none of these . . . .   ( )a ( )b ( )c ( )d

16. Tight monetary policy resulting in higher interest rates will usually have all of the following effects on the economy except **(a)** increased unemployment **(b)** reduced aggregate demand **(c)** increased demand for houses **(d)** reduced rates of inflation . . .   ( )a ( )b ( )c ( )d

17. Under a tight monetary policy with high interest rates, you could reasonably expect individuals to reduce their purchases of **(a)** automobiles **(b)** large consumer appliances such as refrigerators or stereo equipment **(c)** most items that might require them to borrow money to finance the purchases **(d)** all of these. . . . .   ( )a ( )b ( )c ( )d

18. In recent years, it has sometimes seemed that monetary policy does not work at all because interest rates fell during periods of tight monetary policy. This occurred because **(a)** both money supply and demand were changing at the same time **(b)** economists have no knowledge of how the economy works in regard to money **(c)** the Federal Reserve System followed incorrect fiscal policy **(d)** commercial banks set the required reserve ratio too high. . . . .   ( )a ( )b ( )c ( )d

Taxes

Part 1 — Building Your Economic Vocabulary

Directions: Complete each of the following sentences with chapter vocabulary from the list below:

ability-to-pay principle of taxation   progressive tax
benefit principle of taxation   property tax
corporate income tax   proportional tax
direct tax   regressive tax
estate and gift taxes   sales tax
excise tax   social security tax
indirect tax   tax
personal income tax

1. A charge imposed by the government on people or property for public purposes is a
   _____.

2. The concept that those who benefit from the spending of tax dollars should pay the taxes to
   provide those benefits is the _____.

3. The _____ means that those who can best afford to pay taxes
   should pay most of the taxes.

4. A _____ takes a larger percentage of higher incomes and a smaller percentage
   of lower incomes.

5. A tax that takes a larger percentage of lower incomes and a smaller percentage of higher
   incomes is a _____.

6. A _____ takes the same percentage of income from all taxpayers.

7. A tax paid by the person against whom the tax is levied is a _____.

8. A tax that can be shifted, at least in part, to a party other than the one on whom the tax is
   levied is an _____.

9. _____ is a tax on the income of individuals.

10. _____ is a tax on the earnings of corporations.

11. A _____ is a tax on goods that are bought.

12. An _____ is a tax on specific items.

13. A tax levied on real estate such as a home, land, and buildings is a _____.

14. _____ is a tax that provides disability and retirement benefits for most working people.

15. _____ are taxes levied on wealth (money and property) passed from one person to another either at death or as a gift.

Part 2 — Checking Your Economic Knowledge

Directions: Carefully read the following statements. Decide whether each of the following statements is *True* or *False*. Fill in the answer bubble with **T** for *True* or **F** for *False*. If any part of the statement is *False*, then the statement is *False*.

1. Although the specific uses of tax revenues vary a great deal, it is safe to say that taxes are levied primarily to pay the costs of government. . . . .   ( )T ( )F

2. Taxes are frequently used by government to provide public goods, correct problems caused by market failures, and to stabilize the economy. . . . .   ( )T ( )F

3. Most of the tax revenues received by the federal government come from taxes levied on corporate profits.. . . . .   ( )T ( )F

4. The federal government spends the largest part of its revenues on national defense.. . . . .   ( )T ( )F

5. An example of the benefit principle of taxation is the U.S. personal income tax because the higher your taxable income is, the higher your marginal tax rate is. . . . .   ( )T ( )F

6. An example of the ability-to-pay principle of taxation is the use of the revenues from taxes on gasoline to build and maintain roads.. . . . .   ( )T ( )F

7. If everyone had to pay 10 percent of his or her taxable income as personal income tax, this would be a proportional tax. . . . .   ( )T ( )F

8. When a corporation can shift the burden of a tax onto consumers through charging higher prices, the tax is an indirect tax.. . . . .   ( )T ( )F

9. A company's tax base is determined by adding certain business expenses to its gross income.. . . . .   ( )T ( )F

10. The social security tax is a regressive tax because people above the highest tax base pay the same amount as those who are at the highest tax base. . . . .   ( )T ( )F

Part 3 — Mastering Economic Concepts

Directions: Carefully read the following items. Fill in the answer bubble next to the letter of the *best* answer.

1. The largest portion of all tax revenues collected by the U.S. government comes from **(a)** excise taxes **(b)** corporate income taxes **(c)** social security taxes **(d)** individual income taxes . . . .   ( )a ( )b ( )c ( )d

2. The U.S. government spends the largest portion of its revenues on **(a)** interest on the public debt **(b)** health and income security **(c)** national defense **(d)** education and training programs . . . .   ( )a ( )b ( )c ( )d

3. State governments receive the largest part of their tax revenues from **(a)** sales taxes **(b)** excise taxes **(c)** property taxes **(d)** corporate income taxes. . . . .   ( )a ( )b ( )c ( )d

4. The largest source of tax revenues for local governments such as those of towns and cities is **(a)** personal income taxes **(b)** corporate income taxes **(c)** property taxes **(d)** license fees. . . . .   ( )a ( )b ( )c ( )d

5. The largest single type of expenditure that state and local governments make is for **(a)** police protection **(b)** parks and recreation **(c)** public housing **(d)** education . . . .   ( )a ( )b ( )c ( )d

6. The benefit principle of taxation is based on the idea that a tax should be paid by **(a)** those who are most able to pay **(b)** those who receive the benefits that the tax revenues provide **(c)** all citizens regardless of whether they receive benefits or not **(d)** only those citizens receiving social security benefits . . . .   ( )a ( )b ( )c ( )d

7. The ability-to-pay principle of taxation is based on the idea that a tax should be paid by **(a)** those who have the ability to receive the benefits of the tax **(b)** those who have the greatest ability to pay the tax in terms of their income **(c)** every citizen regardless of income or benefits received **(d)** all of these . . . .   ( )a ( )b ( )c ( )d

8. A progressive tax is a tax that **(a)** takes larger portions of higher incomes **(b)** takes smaller portions of higher incomes **(c)** takes an equal portion of income at all levels **(d)** is progressive in that it looks more toward the future than the present in terms of revenues . . . .   ( )a ( )b ( )c ( )d

9. A regressive tax is a tax that takes **(a)** a smaller percentage of lower incomes and a higher percentage of higher incomes **(b)** a higher percentage of all incomes **(c)** a higher percentage of lower incomes and a lower percentage of higher incomes **(d)** an equal percentage of all incomes . . . .   ( )a ( )b ( )c ( )d

10. A proportional tax is one that **(a)** takes the same percentage of income from all taxpayers **(b)** takes proportionally higher percentages of higher incomes **(c)** taxes only a fixed proportion of the taxpayers in the economy **(d)** provides equal benefits for all who pay the tax. . . . .   ( )a ( )b ( )c ( )d

11. When economists refer to *tax incidence,* they are talking about **(a)** how frequently the tax is used in the economy **(b)** whether the tax coincides with the income of those who pay the tax **(c)** who actually pays the tax **(d)** none of these. . . . .   ( )a ( )b ( )c ( )d

12. A direct tax is one that is paid by **(a)** the individual against whom it is levied **(b)** a party other than the individual it is levied against **(c)** the government **(d)** the directors of the corporation against which it is levied. . . . .   ( )a ( )b ( )c ( )d

13. An indirect tax is a tax that **(a)** cannot be shifted to another party **(b)** can be shifted to another party **(c)** is indirectly related to the benefit provided by the tax **(d)** all of these. . . . .   ( )a ( )b ( )c ( )d

14. The federal personal income tax in the United States is a
(a) progressive tax **(b)** regressive tax **(c)** proportional tax **(d)** all
of these. . . . .   ( )a ( )b ( )c ( )d

15. Under the present U.S. personal income tax system, if you earned
an additional $20, your total take-home pay could **(a)** be less
than it was before because you might have moved to a higher
tax bracket **(b)** increase by some amount smaller than $20
depending on your individual income tax bracket **(c)** be
unchanged by the additional $20 earned **(d)** all of these . . . .   ( )a ( )b ( )c ( )d

16. The U.S. corporate income tax is **(a)** an indirect tax **(b)** a direct tax
(c) a basically proportional tax **(d)** both (a) and (c) . . . .   ( )a ( )b ( )c ( )d

17. An excise tax on gasoline is an example of **(a)** the benefit
principle of taxation **(b)** a tax that is earmarked **(c)** both (a) and
(b) **(d)** none of these . . . .   ( )a ( )b ( )c ( )d

18. Both excise and sales taxes have the effect of **(a)** increasing price
and reducing quantity demanded **(b)** reducing price and
increasing quantity demanded **(c)** leaving price and quantity
unchanged **(d)** reducing quantity demanded and price . . . .   ( )a ( )b ( )c ( )d

19. Property taxes are an example of taxes that are **(a)** generally
regressive **(b)** not directly related to the taxpayer's income
(c) used most often by local governments **(d)** all of these. . . . .   ( )a ( )b ( )c ( )d

20. Social security taxes and benefits are **(a)** paid by both the
employee and the employer **(b)** a problem for society because
more is paid out than is taken in **(c)** regressive for taxpayers who
earn incomes above the maximum level on which the tax is based
(d) all of these . . . .   ( )a ( )b ( )c ( )d

Fiscal Policy

Part 1 — Building Your Economic Vocabulary

Directions: Match the following terms with the definitions below.

A. budget deficit
B. crowding out
C. expansionary fiscal policies
D. external debt
E. fiscal policy
F. inflationary bias in fiscal policy

G. inside time lag
H. multiplier effect
I. national debt
J. outside time lag
K. restrictive fiscal policies
L. wage and price controls

_____ **1.** the changing of federal government spending and taxes in order to control the level of economic activity

_____ **2.** fiscal policies that cause the economy to run more rapidly by increasing aggregate demand

_____ **3.** the concept that any change in fiscal policy affects total demand and total income by an amount larger than the original amount of the change in spending or taxing

_____ **4.** fiscal policies that cause the economy to run more slowly by reducing aggregate demand

_____ **5.** the amount by which federal government spending exceeds revenues in each year

_____ **6.** the amount of money that the federal government owes

_____ **7.** the effect on private businesses when increased government borrowing raises interest rates and reduces private borrowing

_____ **8.** the part of the national debt that is owned by people or governments outside the United States

_____ **9.** the natural tendency for Congress to favor expansionary policies over restrictive policies

_____ **10.** the time it takes to decide on a policy

_____ **11.** the time it takes for the effects of policy change to be completely felt in the economy

_____ **12.** government controls on the levels of wages and prices

Directions: Carefully read the following statements. Decide whether each of the following statements is *True* or *False*. Fill in the answer bubble for **T** for *True* or **F** for *False*. If any part of the statement is *False,* then the statement is *False.*

1. Fiscal policy is concerned with government spending and taxation while monetary policy is concerned with controlling the supply of money. . . . .   ( )T ( )F

2. Expansionary fiscal policy affects the economy by decreasing aggregate demand. . . . .   ( )T ( )F

3. A decrease in government spending usually reduces income in the economy by more than the amount of the change in government spending, which is an example of the multiplier effect. . . . .   ( )T ( )F

4. Restrictive fiscal policy can be achieved by increasing taxes or reducing government spending to reduce aggregate demand.   ( )T ( )F

5. In general, an expansionary fiscal policy would be used to reduce the level of unemployment. . . . .   ( )T ( )F

6. Restrictive fiscal policy would probably be recommended to reduce the rate of inflation. . . . .   ( )T ( )F

7. Restrictive fiscal policy generally promotes economic growth better than does expansionary fiscal policy . . . .   ( )T ( )F

8. One of the largest drawbacks of fiscal policy is that it has a very long outside time lag. . . . .   ( )T ( )F

9. Fiscal policy is probably more effective than monetary policy in getting the economy out of a recession. . . . .   ( )T ( )F

10. In the history of the U.S. economy, wage and price controls have been effective in reducing inflation and unemployment. . . . .   ( )T ( )F

Part 3 — Mastering Economic Concepts

Directions: Carefully read the following items. Fill in the answer bubble next to the letter of the *best* answer.

1. Fiscal policy involves the changing of **(a)** the supply of money **(b)** the required reserve ratio set by the Federal Reserve **(c)** government spending and taxation to control the amount of economic activity **(d)** none of these . . . .   ( )a ( )b ( )c ( )d

2. Expansionary fiscal policies are policies that bring about **(a)** an increase in aggregate demand **(b)** a decrease in aggregate demand **(c)** a change in the money supply **(d)** all of these . . . .   ( )a ( )b ( )c ( )d

3. Expansionary fiscal policies would include all of the following except **(a)** an increase in government spending on roads and schools **(b)** a reduction in the individual income tax **(c)** the removal of the tax deduction permitted for interest paid by families on a home mortgage **(d)** an increase in government spending on the space program. . . . .   ( )a ( )b ( )c ( )d

4. Restrictive fiscal policies would include all of the following except **(a)** a tax decrease on corporate profits **(b)** a reduction of government spending for national defense **(c)** an increase in the tax rate paid on capital gains **(d)** a reduction in the rate at which the government taxes individual incomes . . . . ( )a ( )b ( )c ( )d

5. In comparing expansionary and restrictive fiscal policies, in general it is safe to say that **(a)** expansionary policy tends to increase income **(b)** restrictive policy tends to increase unemployment **(c)** restrictive policy tends to reduce aggregate demand **(d)** all of these . . . . ( )a ( )b ( )c ( )d

6. The national debt is **(a)** the amount by which federal government spending exceeds revenues in each year **(b)** the amount of money that the federal government owes **(c)** the amount that is owed to people or governments outside the United States **(d)** none of these. . . . . ( )a ( )b ( )c ( )d

7. All of the following are owed part of the national debt except **(a)** the Federal Reserve Banks **(b)** individual U.S. citizens **(c)** foreign governments **(d)** the U.S. military. . . . . ( )a ( )b ( )c ( )d

8. The effect of private businesses being unable to borrow because of high interest rates caused by government borrowing is called **(a)** the crowding-out effect **(b)** the crowd effect **(c)** inflationary bias **(d)** none of these. . . . . ( )a ( )b ( )c ( )d

9. If you were the president of the United States facing a period of high demand deficiency unemployment, you would most likely **(a)** reduce federal income taxes **(b)** increase taxes to pay off the national debt **(c)** reduce government spending on job training programs **(d)** none of these . . . . ( )a ( )b ( )c ( )d

10. If there is a high rate of inflation, the appropriate fiscal policy might be to **(a)** increase taxes **(b)** increase government spending **(c)** reduce taxes **(d)** both reduce taxes and increase government spending. . . . . ( )a ( )b ( )c ( )d

11. In general, the type of fiscal policy that encourages economic growth is **(a)** slightly expansionary **(b)** one that maintains only a mild rate of inflation **(c)** both (a) and (b) **(d)** none of these . . . . . . ( )a ( )b ( )c ( )d

12. Other than controlling inflation and unemployment, the government can encourage economic growth by **(a)** asking businesses to try to grow faster **(b)** providing investment tax credits for businesses to buy new plants and equipment **(c)** increasing the cost of investing in business **(d)** all of these . . . . ( )a ( )b ( )c ( )d

13. The time it usually takes for the president and Congress to agree on fiscal policy is called the **(a)** outside time lag **(b)** inside time lag **(c)** inflationary bias **(d)** none of these . . . . ( )a ( )b ( )c ( )d

14. The time it takes for an agreed-on fiscal policy to be implemented and have an effect on the economy is called the **(a)** outside time lag **(b)** inside time lag **(c)** inflationary bias **(d)** none of these . . . . ( )a ( )b ( )c ( )d

15. The fact that politicians generally favor increased government spending and oppose tax increases is referred to by economists as the **(a)** deflationary tendency of fiscal policy **(b)** the fallacy of government **(c)** the inflationary bias in fiscal policy **(d)** fiscal integrity . . . . ( )a ( )b ( )c ( )d

16. Compared to monetary policy, fiscal policy has **(a)** a shorter outside time lag **(b)** a longer inside time lag **(c)** both (a) and (b) **(d)** none of these . . . . ( )a ( )b ( )c ( )d

17. Wage and price controls are attempts by the government to **(a)** control the rate of inflation **(b)** control the rate of unemployment **(c)** reduce the power of unions to raise wages more than is desirable **(d)** all of these . . . . ( )a ( )b ( )c ( )d

18. When there is a shortage, **(a)** illegal markets usually develop **(b)** rich and powerful people usually end up with the limited amount of the good **(c)** the government might use ration coupons **(d)** all of these . . . . ( )a ( )b ( )c ( )d

Economic Growth

Part 1 — Building Your Economic Vocabulary

Directions: Match the following terms with the definitions below.

A. capital
B. depression
C. economic growth
D. human resources
E. natural resources
F. rate of growth

G. real GDP
H. real GDP per person
I. research and development
J. technology
K. work ethic

_____ **1.** the change in the level of economic activity from one year to another

_____ **2.** the value of gross domestic product after taking out the effect of price changes

_____ **3.** the percentage change in the level of economic activity from one year to the next

_____ **4.** a severe and prolonged decline in the level of economic activity

_____ **5.** the real value of the total output of goods and services divided by the number of people in the economy

_____ **6.** the total raw materials supplied by nature

_____ **7.** the people who work or may be able to work

_____ **8.** goods that are produced and can be used as inputs for further production

_____ **9.** the body of knowledge that is used for the production of goods and services

_____ **10.** the activities undertaken to find new and more efficient methods of production

_____ **11.** the belief that people should work hard and pull their own weight in economic life

Part 2 — Checking Your Economic Knowledge

Directions: Carefully read the following statements. Decide whether the statement is *True* or *False*. Fill in the answer bubble for **T** for *True* or **F** for *False*. If any part of the statement is *False,* then the statement is *False.*

1. Current dollar GDP is a better measure of economic growth than is real GDP. . . .   ( )T ( )F

2. Over the past year, both the GDP and the population of Country A have doubled. Prices have increased by 10 percent. From this information, we can assume that Country A has experienced no economic growth. . . . .   ( )T ( )F

3. A difference in the growth rate between two countries of only 1 percent can mean a very large difference in their GDPs over a 20-year period. . . . .   ( )T ( )F

4. Real GDP is often used to consider the effects of population growth on economic well-being. . . . .   ( )T ( )F

5. The major sources of economic growth are natural and human resources, capital, and technology. . . . .   ( )T ( )F

6. One major improvement in the human resources of the U.S. economy over the last 50 years has been the large increase in the average years of education each citizen has completed.. . . . .   ( )T ( )F

7. The U.S. economy has become more capital intensive over the last 40 years. The use of capital replaces people with machines, reducing the productivity of labor.. . . . .   ( )T ( )F

8. A growing rate of investment contributes to economic growth.. . . . .   ( )T ( )F

9. A growth in the technology of an economy means that the economy can produce more and better quality goods and services at the same or even lower costs. . . . .   ( )T ( )F

10. A positive work ethic means that people want to be productive and contribute to the economy. . . . .   ( )T ( )F

Part 3 — Mastering Economic Concepts

Directions: Carefully read the following items. Fill in the answer bubble next to the letter of the *best* answer.

1. Economic growth is usually measured in terms of growth in real GDP because **(a)** economists have a clear picture of what is real and what is not **(b)** it adjusts for the possible increase in the population **(c)** it adjusts for increases in GDP due to increases in prices without increases in the quantities produced **(d)** it adjusts for the quality of goods and services produced. . . . .   ( )a ( )b ( )c ( )d

2. If Countries A and B have equal GDP today and Country A grows at 2.5 percent per year and Country B at 4.5 percent per year, then in 20 years **(a)** the GDP of the two countries will be about the same **(b)** the GDP of Country B will be significantly larger than that of Country A **(c)** the GDP of Country A will be significantly larger than that of Country B **(d)** none of these . . . . .   ( )a ( )b ( )c ( )d

3. Over the last five years, the GDP of Country A has increased by 50 percent while the price level has increased by 45 percent; therefore, Country A has experienced **(a)** positive real economic growth per person **(b)** negative real economic growth per person **(c)** positive real economic growth **(d)** no change in economic growth . . . .   ( )a ( )b ( )c ( )d

4.

Year	GNP	Price Index	Population
1979	$1.0 billion	1.00	1.0 million
1981	1.25 billion	1.25	1.1 million

Using the data above, you can conclude that for Country A **(a)** there was no increase in real GDP **(b)** real GDP per person decreased **(c)** both (a) and (b) **(d)** none of these . . . .   ( )a ( )b ( )c ( )d

5. Good economic growth was experienced in the United States during the **(a)** 1930s **(b)** 1940s **(c)** 1960s **(d)** 1970s . . . .   ( )a ( )b ( )c ( )d

6. If a candidate for president promises an economic growth rate of 20 percent per year, your most logical reaction will be to **(a)** support this candidate because he or she can bring prosperity to your country **(b)** look for another candidate because that growth rate is probably impossible **(c)** refuse to believe any politician who claims to have knowledge of economic matters **(d)** none of these . . . .   ( )a ( )b ( )c ( )d

7. To see the effect that the growth in real GDP was having on the economic well-being of the population, you might compute growth in **(a)** current dollar GDP **(b)** real GDP per person **(c)** population **(d)** per capita taxation . . . .   ( )a ( )b ( )c ( )d

8. The rate at which an economy can grow is limited by all of the following *except* the **(a)** amount and quality of labor available in the economy **(b)** amount and quality of natural resources in an economy **(c)** amount of capital equipment and technological improvements in an economy **(d)** number of firms producing a certain product in the economy. . . . .   ( )a ( )b ( )c ( )d

9. Over time, as an economy makes use of its natural resources, the cost of those resources can be expected to **(a)** decrease since the economy will grow **(b)** decrease as those resources become more scarce **(c)** stay about the same **(d)** increase as those resources become more scarce. . . . .   ( )a ( )b ( )c ( )d

10. The human resources of the U.S. economy have been able to contribute so much toward its economic growth in the last five decades because the **(a)** educational level of the population has increased a great deal **(b)** size of the population has increased **(c)** skills of the population have increased **(d)** all of these. . . . .   ( )a ( )b ( )c ( )d

11. One factor that makes labor in the U.S. economy so productive relative to labor in many other world economies is that the **(a)** number of laborers available is very high **(b)** health of the workforce is very good **(c)** amount of capital utilized by each employee is high **(d)** people in the United States like to work . . . .   ( )a ( )b ( )c ( )d

12. The rate of investment can be increased by **(a)** reducing the level of inflation **(b)** reducing interest rates **(c)** both (a) and (b) **(d)** increasing interest rates . . . . ( )a ( )b ( )c ( )d ●

13. The largest single source of economic growth in the U.S. economy from 1929 to 1969 was **(a)** improvements in technology **(b)** increases in the size of the population **(c)** improved resource allocation **(d)** reduced taxes. . . . . ( )a ( )b ( )c ( )d

14. Research and development is very important to economic growth because it **(a)** brings about the development of new technologies that can lead to increased productivity **(b)** provides increased employment for scientists **(c)** employs workers who pay taxes **(d)** none of these . . . . ( )a ( )b ( )c ( )d

15. In order to increase the rate of capital investment, an economy must **(a)** print more money **(b)** give up more present consumption **(c)** increase present consumption more than production **(d)** hold consumption constant and decrease savings . . . . ( )a ( )b ( )c ( )d

16. Economic growth is shown on the production possibilities graph as **(a)** a movement along the production possibilities curve from one point to another **(b)** an inward shift of the production possibilities curve **(c)** an outward shift of the production possibilities curve **(d)** none of these. . . . . ( )a ( )b ( )c ( )d

17. Social attitudes in our economy have had some impact on economic growth because **(a)** the American economy has a strong work ethic **(b)** successful businesspeople, inventors, and innovators enjoy positions of high esteem in our society **(c)** most people do not expect to get something for nothing **(d)** all of these. . . . . ( )a ( )b ( )c ( )d ●

18. The government tries to encourage economic growth by **(a)** increasing federal spending for research and development **(b)** implementing tax incentives **(c)** maintaining a loose monetary policy **(d)** all of these . . . . ( )a ( )b ( )c ( )d

●

Name _____   Class _____   Date _____

The Global Marketplace

Part 1 — Building Your Economic Vocabulary

Directions: Match the following terms with the definitions below.

A. absolute advantage
B. balance of payments
C. balance of trade
D. comparative advantage
E. European Community (EC)
F. exchange rate
G. exports
H. flexible exchange rates
I. General Agreement on Tariffs and Trade (GATT)

J. gold standard
K. imports
L. International Monetary Fund (IMF)
M. North American Free Trade Agreement (NAFTA)
N. protectionism
O. quota
P. tariff
Q. trade deficit
R. trade surplus

_____ **1.** goods and services that one country sells to another country

_____ **2.** goods and services that one country buys from another country

_____ **3.** a group of European countries that have joined together and agreed on ways to improve trade among themselves

_____ **4.** the principle that a country benefits from specializing in the production at which it is relatively most efficient

_____ **5.** what one country has when it can produce a good more efficiently than can another country

_____ **6.** a tax on imports

_____ **7.** a limit on the amount of imports or exports

_____ **8.** the idea that we should limit international trade to protect our own self-interest

_____ **9.** an agreement that gave broad international support to improving trade among countries

_____ **10.** a trade agreement established between the United States, Canada, and Mexico to promote economic growth and prosperity for all three economies by eliminating barriers to free trade

_____ **11.** a system in which each nation sets the value of its money in terms of a certain amount of gold

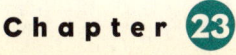

_____ **12.** the result when a country imports more than it exports

_____ **13.** the result when a country exports more than it imports

_____ **14.** a bank established to promote economic cooperation by maintaining an orderly system of world trade and exchange rates

_____ **15.** the rate at which one kind of money can be traded for another

_____ **16.** a system in which the laws of supply and demand set the prices, or exchange rates, between each kind of money

_____ **17.** the level of merchandise exports minus the level of merchandise imports

_____ **18.** the total flow of money coming into a country minus the total flow of money going out of a country

Part 2 — Checking Your Economic Knowledge

Directions: Carefully read the following statements. Decide whether each of the following statements is _True_ or _False._ Fill in the answer bubble for **T** for _True_ or **F** for _False._ If any part of the statement is _False,_ then the statement is _False._

1. About half of U.S. exports go to countries in the European Community. . . . . ( )T ( )F

2. If the United States can produce both computers and televisions more cheaply than can Portugal, it will never be beneficial for the United States to specialize and trade with Portugal. . . . . ( )T ( )F

3. The law of comparative advantage shows that two countries could gain if each specialized in making the good for which it has the comparative advantage. . . . ( )T ( )F

4. If only a specific limited amount of oil may be imported into the United States each year, there is a quota on oil. . . . . ( )T ( )F

5. If we do not restrict world trade, the United States will not be able to have a highly diversified economy. . . . . ( )T ( )F

6. Unions generally want to restrict trade to keep employment in the United States at high levels. . . . . ( )T ( )F

7. A reduction in barriers to free trade such as quotas and tariffs would lower the prices of imports to U.S. consumers. . . . . ( )T ( )F

8. A trade deficit occurs when a country exports more than it imports. . . . . ( )T ( )F

9. A trade surplus occurs when a country imports more than it exports. . . . . ( )T ( )F

10. Flexible exchange rates link the value of a country's currency to the amount of gold it has. . . . . ( )T ( )F

Part 3 — Mastering Economic Concepts

Directions: Carefully read the following items. Fill in the answer bubble next to the letter of the *best* answer.

1. In the U.S. economy, exports presently account for about
   (a) 50 percent of GDP **(b)** 30 percent of GDP **(c)** 15 percent of
   GDP **(d)** 10 percent of GDP. . . . .   ( )a ( )b ( )c ( )d

2. The major U.S. exports include all of the following *except*
   (a) chemicals **(b)** motor vehicles **(c)** grain **(d)** petroleum products. .   ( )a ( )b ( )c ( )d

3. The major U.S. imports include all of the following *except*
   (a) petroleum **(b)** grain **(c)** automobiles **(d)** textiles, clothing, and
   footwear. . . . .   ( )a ( )b ( )c ( )d

4. The main reason nations trade with each other is **(a)** to keep
   good political ties **(b)** the law of comparative advantage **(c)** the
   first law of demand **(d)** none of these . . . .   ( )a ( )b ( )c ( )d

5. The United States is a major exporter of chemicals and Japan is a
   major exporter of automobiles. It is to the advantage of both the
   United States and Japan to specialize and trade chemicals for
   automobiles if **(a)** the United States has a lower opportunity cost
   to produce chemicals than does Japan **(b)** Japan has a higher
   opportunity cost to produce autos than does the United States
   (c) Japan has a lower opportunity cost of producing autos than
   does the United States **(d)** both (a) and (c) . . . .   ( )a ( )b ( )c ( )d

6. When a government places a tax on the import of certain goods,
   it is creating a **(a)** quota **(b)** tariff **(c)** poll tax **(d)** foreign bill of
   exchange . . . .   ( )a ( )b ( )c ( )d

7. When a government sets some limit on the quantity of a good
   that can be imported into the country, it is creating a **(a)** flexible
   exchange rate **(b)** tariff **(c)** quota **(d)** gold standard . . . .   ( )a ( )b ( )c ( )d

8. The major arguments in favor of trade restrictions include all of
   the following *except* **(a)** they protect our national security and
   our infant industries **(b)** they help the United States keep a
   diversified economy **(c)** they protect U.S. workers from
   competition by cheap foreign labor **(d)** they make foreign goods
   cheaper to U.S. consumers . . . .   ( )a ( )b ( )c ( )d

9. In general, it is safe to say that economists **(a)** strongly favor
   trade restrictions **(b)** favor free trade **(c)** have no opinion on
   trade or trade restrictions **(d)** favor trade restrictions only for the
   European Community. . . . .   ( )a ( )b ( )c ( )d

10. In general, restrictions on foreign trade have all of the following
    effects *except* **(a)** they increase the price of goods and services
    that are imported **(b)** they reduce the supply of foreign goods
    (c) they sometimes lead to the misallocation of resources **(d)** they
    make it possible for U.S. citizens to acquire foreign goods at
    prices below what they would pay if the goods were produced
    in the United States . . . .   ( )a ( )b ( )c ( )d

11. The General Agreement on Tariffs and Trade (GATT) is an agreement for **(a)** countries to work together to lower the barriers to free trade **(b)** countries to work together to increase the use of tariffs, quotas, and import taxes **(c)** the United States to ban foreign goods and services from their import markets **(d)** all of these . . . . ( )a ( )b ( )c ( )d

12. Which of the following was formed to encourage international trade? **(a)** North American Trade Community **(b)** European Free Trade Agreement **(c)** European Community **(d)** none of these . . . . ( )a ( )b ( )c ( )d

13. The North American Free Trade Agreement was established **(a)** to eliminate barriers to foreign trade **(b)** between the United States, Canada, and Mexico **(c)** both (a) and (b) **(d)** none of these . . . . ( )a ( )b ( )c ( )d

14. When countries operate on a gold standard, they **(a)** use gold instead of paper money **(b)** set the value of their currencies in terms of a specific amount of gold **(c)** create standards by which gold is made into jewelry **(d)** none of these . . . . ( )a ( )b ( )c ( )d

15. On a gold standard, countries cannot print more money than they have gold to back the money, which is a problem when **(a)** there is a trade surplus that could lead to higher inflation **(b)** there is a trade deficit that could lead to lower aggregate demand and higher unemployment **(c)** both (a) and (b) **(d)** none of these . . . . ( )a ( )b ( )c ( )d

16. The Bretton Woods Agreement of 1944 established **(a)** the U.S. dollar as the key international currency **(b)** gold as the international standard of exchange **(c)** the General Agreement on Tariffs and Trade **(d)** both (a) and (b) . . . . ( )a ( )b ( )c ( )d

17. A system of flexible exchange rates is one in which **(a)** the exchange rate (price) is set by the laws of supply and demand in the marketplace **(b)** market prices for goods and services change in regard to the price of gold **(c)** the amount of goods that two countries trade is based on the amount of gold each has **(d)** all of these. . . . . ( )a ( )b ( )c ( )d

Economic Development: A Global Economic Issue

Part 1 — Building Your Economic Vocabulary

Directions: Complete each of the following sentences with chapter vocabulary from the list below.

barriers to economic development
dual economy
foreign aid
infant mortality rate
less-developed country
life expectancy
population explosion
World Bank

1. Generally, a _____ is defined as a poor country with a relatively low level of education and a largely rural population.

2. The _____ is measured as the number of deaths of children under one year of age per 1,000 live births.

3. The _____ is the average age the people in a country reach.

4. A _____ is one in which a modern market economy exists side by side with a primitive subsistence economy.

5. _____ is the money that more advanced countries provide to help less-developed countries in their economic development.

6. Economic, social, and political characteristics that prevent an economy from developing are called _____.

7. Rapid growth in the number of people living in a country is sometimes referred to as a _____.

8. The _____ was established in 1944 to help finance reconstruction after World War II.

Part 2 — Checking Your Economic Knowledge

Directions: Carefully read the following statements. Decide whether the statement is *True* or *False*. Fill in the answer bubble for **T** for *True* or **F** for *False*. If any part of the statement is *False*, then the statement is *False*.

1. A country that has a relatively low level of education and a largely rural population is referred to as a less-developed or second-world country. . . . .   ( )T ( )F

2. Colombia, Sudan, Tanzania, and Turkey are less-developed countries. . . . .   ( )T ( )F

3. Densely populated countries are less-developed countries. . . . .   ( )T ( )F

4. Infant mortality rate is measured as the number of deaths of children under one year of age per 100 live births. . . . .   ( )T ( )F

5. People who live in less-developed countries have low levels of health care resulting in low life expectancies and high infant mortality. . . . .   ( )T ( )F

6. There is an opportunity cost to those more-advanced countries who provide foreign aid. . . . .   ( )T ( )F

7. Human capital is the amount of money each person has in a country. . . . .   ( )T ( )F

8. The higher the rate of population growth, other things being equal, the more difficult it is to launch and sustain a process of economic development. . . . .   ( )T ( )F

9. Foreign aid exists solely to soften the threat to the national security of an advanced country, because of the widening gap between rich and poor nations. . . . .   ( )T ( )F

10. The purpose of the World Bank includes assistance to less-developed countries, but, at the time of the Bretton Woods Agreement in 1944, the reconstruction of war-devastated areas was the foremost consideration. . . . .   ( )T ( )F

Part 3 — Mastering Economic Concepts

Directions: Carefully read the following items. Fill in the answer bubble next to the letter of the *best* answer.

1. Countries are considered to be less developed if their level of income per person is **(a)** less than $3,000 per year **(b)** more than $3,000 per year **(c)** $5,000 per year **(d)** $6,000 per year . . . .   ( )a ( )b ( )c ( )d

2. If we are to rely on a single indicator of the level of development of a particular country, what will be the most revealing? **(a)** Real GNP per person **(b)** Balance of trade **(c)** Mortality rate **(d)** Population. . . . .   ( )a ( )b ( )c ( )d

3. Kenya, Nigeria, Sri Lanka, and Tanzania **(a)** all have GNP per person below $1,000 **(b)** have political structures that include institutionalized bureaucracy **(c)** are less-developed countries **(d)** both (a) and (c) . . . .   ( )a ( )b ( )c ( )d

4. Less-developed countries are characterized by **(a)** large and increasing gaps in productivity and income among major groups **(b)** low life expectancy and high infant mortality rate **(c)** rapid population growth **(d)** all of these. . . . .   ( )a ( )b ( )c ( )d

5. Life expectancy is generally defined as **(a)** the average age the people in a country reach **(b)** the average level of health **(c)** the average age the children in a country reach **(d)** both (b) and (c) ..   ( )a ( )b ( )c ( )d

6. The poor getting poorer and the rich getting richer results in the existence of a **(a)** dual economy **(b)** modern market economy **(c)** subsistence economy **(d)** none of the above . . . .   ( )a ( )b ( )c ( )d

7. The low level of income in less-developed countries has an adverse effect on advanced countries because **(a)** opportunity cost exists in that if the buying power of a less-developed country were greater, there would be a larger market to produce for **(b)** failure to repay loans can create instability **(c)** foreign aid to LDCs could be used to solve the domestic problems of the advanced country **(d)** all of these . . . .   ( )a ( )b ( )c ( )d

8. One barrier to economic development is **(a)** limited natural resources **(b)** capitalism **(c)** shortage of investment **(d)** both (a) and (c) . . . .   ( )a ( )b ( )c ( )d

9. Which of the following is not a barrier to economic development? **(a)** Low human capital **(b)** Rapid population growth **(c)** Shortage of investment capital **(d)** None of these . . . . .   ( )a ( )b ( )c ( )d

10. Less-developed countries generally do not have **(a)** a diversity of resources **(b)** limited natural resources **(c)** a favorable political environment **(d)** all of these . . . .   ( )a ( )b ( )c ( )d

11. The skills of the labor force of a less-developed country are often centered on **(a)** agriculture **(b)** politics **(c)** commerce **(d)** all of these . . . .   ( )a ( )b ( )c ( )d

12. A shortage of investment capital exists in LDCs because **(a)** the level of savings is low so less money is available **(b)** LDCs cannot promote development **(c)** of a low level of human skills **(d)** none of these . . . .   ( )a ( )b ( )c ( )d

13. The best hope for economic development must come from **(a)** a political structure that exercises proper governmental action **(b)** rapid population growth **(c)** foreign aid **(d)** none of these . . . .   ( )a ( )b ( )c ( )d

14. An unfavorable political environment is a barrier to economic development because **(a)** political leaders may be corrupt and/or incompetent **(b)** the elite class rules **(c)** the political structure favors the masses **(d)** none of these . . . .   ( )a ( )b ( )c ( )d

15. The World Bank, in order to aid LDCs, borrows from **(a)** wealthy individuals **(b)** leading corporations **(c)** rich nations of the world **(d)** the LDCs themselves . . . .   ( )a ( )b ( )c ( )d

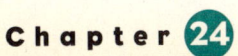